IN THE MIDST OF
THE WHIRLWIND

A MANUAL FOR HELPING
REFUGEE CHILDREN

IN THE MIDST OF THE WHIRLWIND

A MANUAL FOR HELPING REFUGEE CHILDREN

Naomi Richman

Save the Children

tb

City and Hackney Community Services NHS Trust
and Save the Children with
Trentham Books

First published in 1998 by Trentham Books Limited

Trentham Books Limited
Westview House
734 London Road
Oakhill
Stoke on Trent
Staffordshire
England ST4 5NP

British Cataloguing in Publication Data
A catalogue record for this book is available from the British Library
ISBN 1 85856 101 9

Designed and typeset by Trentham Print Design Ltd., Chester and printed in Great Britain by Cromwell Press Ltd, Wiltshire

CONTENTS

SECTION 2
HELPING CHILDREN AND FAMILIES

Chapter 1

INTRODUCTION

Refugee children have been swept from their familiar home to a strange land. Some have escaped from war or oppression relatively unscathed; others have suffered greatly. In their own country they may have lived for many years with tension, violence and oppression; perhaps loved ones have disappeared or died. Their journey to safety could have been long and dangerous, often the most terrifying of all their ordeals. Once arrived they hope for peace and safety; instead they may face uncertainty and insecurity. Asylum is not always assured; living conditions are hard; parents are worried and tense.

In this whirlwind of existence all of us who work with refugee children try to offer a space of calmness and hope, but it is a challenge to respond to them adequately. Often people withdraw from the children because they feel overwhelmed by the complexity of their situation: it seems too much to cope with their suffering, their uncertainty, the obstacles to communication and understanding.

This manual is written with the aim of providing a framework for understanding the situation of refugee children, assessing their difficulties, and making plans to help them. It should provide helpful ideas for those who work with refugees in all settings, including social workers, refugee community groups, health visitors, nursery workers, paediatricians, counsellors, psychologists and psychiatrists. There is a special emphasis on the role of teachers because school plays such a central part in children's well-being.

> For the purpose of this manual, unless stated otherwise, refugee will refer to those who are seeking asylum, or have Exceptional Leave to Remain (ELR) on humanitarian grounds, as well as to those who have full refugee status.

The UN Convention on the Rights of the Child (United Nations Nov, 1989) provides a practical starting point for thinking about the rights of refugee children. It specifies the rights to which children are entitled, and the obligation of the state to promote these rights (Article 4), and to provide adequate care when parents are unable to do so (Articles 3, 20). It upholds, amongst other liberties, the child's right to survival and development (Article 6), to preservation of identity (Article 8), to live with parents (Article 9), to be protected from abuse and neglect (Article 19), and to health care (Article 24). Article 22 provides for the special protection and assistance to children who are refugees or seeking to become so.

Children also have the right to benefit from Social Security (Article 26) and an adequate standard of living (article 27).

Article 29 provides for education that develops the child's personality and talents, and respects the child's own cultural values.

It is also useful when considering the needs of refugee children to ensure that their rights under the 1989 Children Act take precedence over Asylum Law, eg with respect to their rights to education, health care, benefits and housing. This is of particular relevance when considering the right to a family and urging the need for family reunification of a child whose parents are in another country.

The manual starts from the assumption that refugees are survivors who have come through great difficulties: often the adults have risked their lives by challenging oppression. Both adults and children have skills and emotional resources to draw on that must be recognised and used. Although by its nature this book concentrates on the difficulties faced by refugees, it must be emphasised that most show impressive capacities to overcome the challenges they face. However, often their lives would be easier if they received more understanding and support, and some who could be helped suffer alone because they are not reached by relevant services.

I believe that having a 'wait and see' approach before offering support is probably more expensive and time consuming than giving adequate support initially. It is important to be *proactive* and to invest in programmes that *prevent* problems from arising or escalating. There is an opinion that refugees' needs are so complex that special training is required to help them but much preventive work, which should be the cornerstone of support, does not require specialists.

The manual is directed at those who work with children, and this involves being aware of the needs of parents and other carers. Family love and adequate care are what children need most, but this is absent for unaccompanied children who arrive without any responsible adult. Even when adult carers are present, for various reasons they may find it difficult to respond to the children's needs: it is as important to support carers as children.

Many of the problems discussed here are similar to those of other migrants and of poor urban dwellers in general, and many policies and supporting programmes will be similar for all these children. Ideas arising from work with refugees often turn out to be helpful for many children.

Contents of manual

Section 1 of the manual looks at the varied experiences of refugees and how these affect children's development and family life.

Chapter 2 introduces the background to refugees in Britain, how people come to be refugees, issues about gaining asylum, the current social situation of refugees.

Chapter 3 discusses the kinds of experiences undergone by adults and how these affect family relationships and functioning. Disrupted families, losses and separations, adjustment to a new culture, all affect how families manage.

Chapter 4 looks at the impact of past and current experiences on children's development and the factors that influence how they cope with adversity. Changes of carer, loss and separation are especially important to children.

The complex ways in which communities are affected by their experiences and their roles in support are introduced in Chapter 5.

The processes of adaptation to a new society, and the question of identity, are central concerns for both children and adults. The issues of how identity changes in the process of adaptation, and of generational differences in this process are treated in Chapter 6.

The second part of the manual, Section 2, discusses aspects of support for children and families.

Refugees themselves can best explain their predicaments, and good communication is needed with the children and their families in order to understand their concerns, their strengths, and the supports they require. Without good communication it is not possible to understand each other and work out solutions together; this entails overcoming language obstacles and developing trust.

Communication and understanding between refugees and the host community are examined in Chapter 7.

Working skilfully with interpreters is essential but is often a cause of anxiety. Chapter 8 looks at some of the issues affecting this work.

A summary of the various factors that affect children and how they cope with adversity follows in Chapter 9. This leads on to the importance of prevention and implications for how children can be helped.

Although the book is particularly about psychological support it emphasises especially the role of teachers. This is because school plays a pivotal role in adaptation: it is where children learn English and the subtleties of communication in an alien culture, and begin to make friends and enter the social life of their new country. The most helpful event for a child, apart from having loving carers, is to be happily placed in school.

Chapter 10 deals with parents' and children's hopes and puzzlements about school; Chapter 11 with how general school policies contribute to children's security and well-being and promote their learning.

The therapeutic influence of creative and recreational activities is stressed in Chapter 12. These play a role in helping children to express themselves and to come to terms with their experiences, as well as providing opportunities for enjoyment, success and social integration.

Chapter 13 reviews the complexities of assessing refugee children who are having difficulties in learning, or in behaviour at school or at home. The process of assessment is hampered by, amongst other factors, difficulties in communication and lack of tools for assessing language and learning; delays in accessing services contribute to escalating problems.

Chapter 14 describes the kinds of help available for children and families experiencing difficulties, and emphasises the diverse ways in which school can assist.

Although the number of refugee children in contact with social services is not high, those who are are amongst the most vulnerable, especially children who are unaccompanied and in care. Chapter 15 looks at how these children can be supported.

The book should provide helpful ideas for professionals who work with refugees in all settings: teachers, health visitors, social workers, youth workers, psychologists family doctors, paediatricians. It is designed to be used as a basis for discussion and training and there are questions at the end of each section which can be used to explore the issues raised, whether in the form of buzz groups, case discussions, role play or group work. Where possible it is a good idea to base the discussions on actual cases brought by the participants in training sessions.

The cases used to illustrate the various topics are based on real children but with changes of name and detail in order to maintain anonymity.

Acknowledgements

This book arose from a project looking at the needs of refugee children in Hackney, supported by North Thames Regional Health Authority, and London Implementation Zone (Richman, 1996).

The work was initiated in conjunction with Sue Jenkins and Heather Hunt, and I thank them and Deborah Hodes for all their support, and the Community Child and Adolescent Health Department, City and Hackney Community Services NHS Trust where the work was based.

I am grateful to the many refugees, both adult and children, who shared their concerns with me.

I was fortunate to be able to discuss these ideas with colleagues in Hackney and elsewhere. They are too numerous to name all individually but amongst them I would particularly like to mention Funda Kansu, Didem Yurtoglu, Zarha Saeed, Obah Saeed, Vinh Chu, Eleanor Blackman, Dee Beidas, Jale Yezar, Nilgun Ali, Fatmah Atasoy, Nafisa Guleid, Agkul and Cahit Baylav, Janet Richardson, Sheila Kasabova, Ros Finlay, Jill Rutter, Sheila Melzak, Jeremy Woodcock.

Many teachers, especially those with special responsibility for ESOL, contributed their time and ideas and I thank them all.

I am especially indebted to Sheila Melzak for providing the slides used to illustrate the manual. These were taken from drawings done by children attending the Medical Foundation for the Care and Treatment of Victims of Torture for psychotherapy.

SECTION 1
THE EXPERIENCES OF REFUGEES

Chapter 2

BACKGROUND

❏ ASYLUM ISSUES

Under international law people have the right to seek asylum. They will be granted refugee status if they have a well founded fear of being persecuted for reasons of race, religion, nationality, membership of a particular social group, or because of their political opinions. The fear must relate to prospective persecution should they return to the country of origin, not just to past persecution. The rights of asylum seekers are outlined in international law in the 1981 UN Convention Relating to the Rights of Refugees.

The process of applying for asylum is complex and legislation is in a state of flux. Up to date information on asylum law can be obtained from the Refugee Council or the Refugee Legal Centre (see Appendix).

In brief, in response to an asylum application full refugee status or exceptional leave to remain (ELR) on humanitarian grounds may be granted. Compared with full asylum status this latter status has reduced entitlements to benefits, and requests for family reunification are not allowed until some years have elapsed. If the asylum application is rejected an appeal can be made to the Home Office.

The process of making a claim for asylum, waiting for the Home Office decision and, if refused, making an appeal, often takes an extremely long time, possibly several years, during which the refugees remain uncertain of their fate. In recent years Government policy has been to make it increasingly difficult to obtain asylum and the number of refugees granted full asylum status is decreasing. Over 75% of applicants are now refused either refugee status or ELR (Refugee Council, 1997).

The culture of disbelief about the validity of claims and uncertainty about the outcome creates enormous anxiety; in this unsettling situation it is hard to begin the process of adaptation to a new country.

It is illegal to detain in prison young people under the age of 18 years who apply for asylum, but in some cases detention has occurred, because there are doubts about the young person's age or about their story. In these cases young people, usually unaccompanied, are exposed to undesirable conditions which are extremely distressing.

Because they are dealt with under the Children Act it is not always realised that unaccompanied children should make an asylum claim. If this is not done, when they reach the age of 18 years their need for asylum may not be recognised by the Home Office.

It is essential that refugees receive proper legal representation when making their asylum claim. If you think that a family or a young person seeking asylum is not receiving adequate legal help you can refer them to, or yourself contact for advice either the Refugee Council or the Refugee Legal Centre. A list of firms with experience in immigration and asylum matters is available from the Immigration Law Practitioners Association. The Children's Legal Centre represents unaccompanied refugee children in the asylum process (see Appendix).

Special advisers are now available through the Refugee Council to ensure that unaccompanied children receive adequate care and legal advice about asylum issues, when they first arrive in this country. However they do not deal with young people living with relatives. The Panel of Advisers is contactable through the Refugee Council.

❑ BECOMING A REFUGEE

Refugees come from divergent backgrounds with varying experiences and reasons for seeking asylum, and the degree of political involvement varies between and within refugee groups. Many are civilians caught between opposing factions in civil war as in Sierra Leone or Liberia. Others, as in Columbia, find themselves in the midst of conflict between Government and other groups, (guerrillas, insurgents, drug dealers) where neither side allows ordinary people to be neutral and live in peace.

Some refugee groups have been oppressed for years in their own country, forbidden to use their own language like the Kurds, or to practice their religion like the Bahai. In other cases discrimination has resurfaced, as against the Roma in Eastern Europe.

Sometimes years of deprivation and harassment have preceded seeking asylum in Britain, including displacement within their own country, as with Colombians, or forced exile into neighbouring countries, like the Somalis.

I wish we could all live together

Political activists protesting against abuse of human rights by their governments are the people most likely to be detained and tortured, although this can happen to anyone from an oppressed group, perhaps an uninvolved bystander or the relative of an activist, or as part of a policy of intimidation.

The process of fleeing can in itself be fraught with difficulty and danger, and is often the most frightening of all their experiences, eg fleeing by boat, trying to find papers and passport and having to bribe officials to leave the country.

Thus refugees experience various phases of adversity of differing length and severity, including oppression and violence in the country of origin, displacement within the country of origin, flight and exile to a nearby country, flight and exile to the West.

❑ SOCIAL ISSUES

In contrast to some other countries that have settlement programmes, the UK does not have statutory programmes for asylum seekers and refugees, who are very much left to find their own feet. Individual local authority services and voluntary bodies have to respond to these needs with limited resources, and often poorly coordinated services.

Legislation about benefit and rights to housing for asylum seekers is under review, but currently those who apply for asylum *after* they have entered the country, rather than immediately on arrival at the port of entry, are not entitled to benefit unless and until they receive the right to stay. This leads to great hardship and in some cases destitution. Voluntary bodies are increasingly involved in caring for refugees but are hard pressed to respond to the needs of the many waiting for asylum claims to be established.

Even those receiving benefit usually live in poor housing or in bed and breakfast accommodation. Cramped housing and poor conditions such as damp, rats, and noise, add to the strain on the family and have an adverse effect on their health. Lack of money severely limits what can be spent on heating and food.

As their housing is temporary, at least initially, families tend to move frequently. This makes it difficult for them to put down any roots and interferes with continuity of schooling and health care. Parents cannot pay fares to enable the children to continue at the previous school. Vaccinations and medical investigations are not completed, and there is a risk that someone who needs treatment will be lost to follow up. Homeless families in general have poor health, and a further obstacle to health care is that some General Practitioners are reluctant to register people who have no permanent address (Hendessi, 1987, Power et al, 1995). Moves can lead to a child being out of school for long periods because of difficulties in finding a school place.

Accessing services can be difficult because they are scattered, and much time is spent going from one department to another, eg education, housing, social services, and so on, often with long waits at each place. Advice centres and one-stop shops where services are concentrated in one place can ease this burden. Some initiatives provide several services in one place, for example the Hunter Street Health Clinic which has GP sessions, and advice on housing, welfare and education plus interpreters.

❏ FINDING OUT ABOUT REFUGEE COMMUNITIES

It is helpful to know about the social and political conditions in different communities, but this can be daunting when faced with refugees from many countries. Sources of information come from individual refugees themselves, from literature, (the Minority Rights Group produces useful books, only a few which can be mentioned here); from organisations such as Amnesty International, the Refugee Council, the Medical Foundation for Victims of Torture (see Appendix). Refugee community groups are also of course major sources of information (see Africa Watch, 1980, Boman and Edwards, 1984, Dalglish, 1989, Eastmond, 1989, Lewis, 1994, Lin K-M et al, 1982, Loizos, 1982, McDowell, 1982, Samatar, 1991, Rutter, 1994).

Means that have been found useful include

- talking with individual adults and children, using the opportunity to discuss differences between host and migrant cultures

- asking children to write about their lives. If they prefer to write in their own language their writings can then be translated

- holding meetings with members of a local community

- attending refugee cultural events

Some public libraries and school libraries also provide sources of information.

QUESTIONS FOR DISCUSSION

Where do the refugees you are in contact with come from?

What have you found to be the problems facing newly arrived refugee families and children?

How could you find out more about the lives and histories of refugee groups?

14

Chapter 3

FAMILIES

Recent arrivals are faced with acute practical problems but even people who have been in Britain for many years are not always settled. Issues such as unresolved asylum claims, separation from close relatives, poor housing, lack of money, limited English, and isolation may still be causing distress.

Surveys have found that generally adult refugees give priority to settling their practical problems. When asked about major concerns they mention asylum, housing, benefits, health, and separation from close relatives (Carey-Wood *et al*, 1995). They also refer to difficulties in finding work (the majority are unemployed) and, especially for women, in learning English.

Many refugees are well educated and have worked in professional or managerial jobs; however their qualifications are unlikely to be recognised and the majority are unable to find work (Carey-Wood *et al*, 1995).

❑ FAMILY DISRUPTION

Even before leaving their country many families have already experienced moves and disruptions. Perhaps they have not all been living together because the father was detained in prison or had to flee into exile first, or was forced to work abroad. Relationships have to be rebuilt once the family is reunited (Sluzki, 1994, Barudy, 1989, Arroyo and Eth, 1985).

> In one family the father had been forced to flee his country and work abroad; the mother and her three children remained in the country of origin. When they were finally reunited in Britain the mother and children (now teenagers) were resentful about the years of harassment and serious threats they had received in their country. They felt the father had deserted them, even though they knew this was irrational because it had been too dangerous for him to stay, and he had sent them money regularly.
>
> The whole family needed time to acknowledge that everyone had suffered during the separation, and to get used to living together once more. The father had to find his place in the family again, especially difficult as the mother was now used to taking all the decisions on her own.

Not everyone in a family may agree with the political activity of parents that led them to flee their country, and children or a partner may blame the politically active person for the disruption this has caused in their lives and feel considerable anger about this.

Separations

The adults say 'my body is here but my heart is in ..(their home country)'. Refugees feel split in half, as though living in two places and two time frames at once, and continually think about the situation back home and the people left behind. They feel guilty when they are in safety and reasonable comfort, especially if their relatives are in unsafe conditions with limited food and water, and no medical care. In cases where not all the family were able to flee together there is much heartache over absent family, and anxiety over the difficulties of family reunification.

Sometimes it is impossible for mothers to bring their young children with them because there is not enough time to organise the flight or insufficient money for everyone to obtain documents that enable them to flee. If the documents do not contain details on all the children some may have to be left behind.

> Zarha, aged 25, was caring for her three younger brothers who had come into exile with her, but had to leave her own little son behind; she could not be reunited with him because her asylum status was not settled.

When seeking asylum, teenage girls may be given priority by the family when there is risk of rape, or teenage boys sent away in order to avoid forced conscription.

Refugees can apply for family reunion if they have permanent refugee status, but this may take a long time to arrange. Reunion can only be requested for close relatives – usually the parents or children of the applicant. Other relatives may not be considered eligible, eg brothers or sisters of the applicants, and this leads to long and painful separations (Woodcock, 1994).

Contact is often lost between different family members and it is disturbing not to know at least whether someone is still alive. The Red Cross and Red Crescent plus various organisations within countries will help with tracing families.

When reunion does take place it sometimes produces unexpected trials when new arrivals find that their relatives are not as they remember them.

A mother, arriving from Iran to join her 15 year old daughter who had been living in Britain with an aunt for four years, was dismayed to meet a young lady dressed in a mini skirt. The daughter had become accustomed to a new social life and did not welcome her mother's wish to change her back to her former ways.

The 'disappeared'

In many countries people disappear – taken away by police or militias for political reasons and not heard of again, or known to be in prison and then suddenly vanish. There is no record of what has happened to these 'disappeared' people but usually they are killed, and this may come to light much later. The fate of the 'disappeared' causes more pain to relatives than any other situation. They cannot begin a process of mourning until they know what happened, and the existence of impunity, the lack of punishment for those who carry out these killings, affects them deeply (Summerfield, 1995).

The fate of these relatives may emerge years later, as has happened in Argentina where it is now known that many of the 'disappeared' were drugged and thrown out of planes.

❑ CHANGES IN STATUS AND ROLES

In a new country all family members have to adjust to new roles because they cannot live as they did formerly, for example fathers may lose their importance as the breadwinner of the family and as a respected member of the community. They become depressed by their loss of role and diminished status.

A high proportion of refugees are well educated and have skills and professions that could contribute to their own community and the country as a whole. However their qualifications are rarely recognised and generally neither men nor women refugees find work in keeping with the level of their education: those with skills or professions are often unemployed (Carey-Wood *et al*, 1995). Women find (low paid) employment more easily than men. As we know, employment and satisfying work are major sources of well-being; most people become disheartened and lose their self-esteem, when they have nothing to do, and no prospects of work. Activists who no longer have a political role are doubly bereft.

Young people may not realise that their parents deserve respect on account of their struggle for human rights, as parents seldom discuss such political activity with them. They may even think that their parents must have done something wrong to have been imprisoned.

Worry about asylum and about relatives left behind, efforts to deal with housing and other aspects of settling in, place great strain on parents. They may also be distressed because of physical injuries or memories of suffering in the home country.

Relations between the parents is affected by the separations and violence they have experienced. Torture or rape or other painful experiences that are hard to speak about act as a barrier between the couple, affecting their communication and trust and their sexual relationship. Distress in parents can lead to irritability and anger, depression, withdrawal, exhaustion, and physical complaints like nightmares or headaches, and impede their capacity for child care. Parents may be unable to support one another and if they are depressed or preoccupied they may find it hard to respond to their children's needs (Melzak, 1995, Woodcock, 1995).

> A mother's efforts to care for her young children were affected by her depression. She had been detained and raped in her own country and this affected her relationship with her husband so that they were unable to work together in caring for the children. She spent much of the time in bed because she felt so exhausted.

Anger is a frequent response to the frustration of life in exile, anxiety about asylum, and pent-up feelings following torture or experiences of violence. The anger may be expressed by parental rows or be directed at the children.

❏ WOMEN'S LIVES

Women's situation changes enormously if they are living without their husbands and families, and face new responsibilities in a strange land. Some have lost their role as independent working women or political activists. Others are unused to going out alone or amongst strangers. They may be reluctant to go to English classes where there are strangers, or to talk to doctors or teachers who are men, and prefer to attend events where only women are present.

Women who have been raped find it especially difficult to talk to men, and are very concerned about issues of safety. Their lives and their children's lives can become very restricted because of their fears.

The support available in the mother country from kin and neighbours is now absent because they live far away from compatriots or because others are busy with their own affairs. This is particularly so for mothers of young children who are unable to meet friends, work or study because they cannot access child care. However some women manage to organise informal networks of support, providing child care and sometimes loan schemes (Sluzki, 1989).

Although most refugee groups have organised community centres, these are usually run by men and are not always responsive to women's needs. Initiatives exist for helping women to reduce their isolation, informing them about the host society, improving access to English classes and training and introducing them to women from the host society through befriending schemes. They include

- preschool services eg playgroups and kindergartens, often with groups for mothers and English classes

- volunteer befriending schemes for isolated women

- English lessons either with home tutors or in groups in schools, community centres, or libraries, and with creche facilities provide

- group discussions can provide emotional support in a non-threatening environment. Groups focused on mental health are unlikely to be acceptable but those dealing with topics such as health information, nutrition and cooking, relaxation and exercises, are more acceptable. They provide moral support and can lead to explorations of important issues such as domestic violence as participants wish (Blakeney *et al*, 1994, Daycare Trust Report, 1995).

Loncarevic (1996) describes a group for Bosnian women which involved self-defence classes, parenting skills and advocacy, particularly in relation to housing, as well as opportunities for group discussions. The group developed good morale. It supported its members, who grew more confident and became advocates for their community for access to better housing.

Health issues

Women are often worried about their health but have difficulties communicating with health workers. They may come to clinics with their husbands or children to act as interpreters, and this inhibits the consultation especially when gynaecological or emotional problems are concerned (Abdullah and Benjamin, 1995, Kansu, 1997).

Health advocates have played an important role as bicultural workers who are able to mediate between patients and health providers, particularly important for women who are embarrassed when dealing with male health workers. Lack of female health workers, interpreters and advocates limits access to adequate health care for many women (Abdullah and Benjamin, 1995, Kansu, 1997).

Domestic violence

Domestic violence occurs everywhere on the world; it is likely to rise in frequency when the family unit is under strain. Refugee women subject to domestic violence are in a particularly difficult situation. Refugee communities may ostracise those who protest against domestic violence or seek help outside the community, because they believe that these problems should be kept within the family. This is very frightening for women who are dependent on their community for social support and have no contacts outside their own community (Kansu, 1997).

In addition a women whose asylum claim is linked to that of her husband will be afraid of losing that status if she leaves him.

These factors make it particularly difficult for refugee women experiencing violence to seek help, especially when they do not speak English. It is not easy to contact women in need, or to ensure their safety, even if they do manage to find refuge.

QUESTIONS FOR DISCUSSION

What are the stresses impinging on refugee families? How could they be helped?

A Somali mother is living with six children aged between five and thirteen years; her husband was killed in Somalia. She feels burdened by her responsibilities, and is depressed and isolated. What measures would be helpful for her?

Chapter 4

CHILDREN'S LIVES

Adults and children arrive here with diverse experiences and expectations and are affected differently by the challenges of adaptation. Refugee children are faced with trying to make sense of what has happened to them in the past while at the same time adapting to their new situation. They may have suffered violence, loss, separation, family disruption, terrifying journeys. Current concerns may include uncertainty about asylum, worry about the safety of relatives left behind, difficult living conditions, and the challenges of settling into school.

❏ SECONDARY ADVERSITY

There is a tendency to concentrate on children's past and what they experienced before they arrived in this country, but it seems that their circumstances in exile are at least as important for adaptation as previous events. A study of Jewish children who were in hiding during the Holocaust found that decisions taken after the end of war: whether they stayed with their foster parents or went to relatives or to a children's home, strongly affected their subsequent psychological state (Kielson, 1992).

Other studies have shown that for children who receive little support at home, a relationship with an understanding adult (often a teacher) can have a powerful protective effect and enable them to make a more successful life for themselves when they grow up. To unaccompanied children especially, the presence of understanding adults, who give affection and help the children to make sense of their experiences, can be crucial.

Adversity has a cumulative effect. The more difficulties children face the harder it is for them to deal with what has happened to them. A spiral of difficulties occurs when the first events produce secondary adversities, for example if the placement for an unaccompanied child is unsatisfactory. Children placed with foster parents who cannot communicate with them or who find it difficult to respond to their needs or empathise with their culture, enter a new phase of tension. Breakdown of care arrangements with relatives or foster parents can lead to progressive demoralisation and behaviour problems, especially if finding a permanent placement proves impossible.

On the other hand, children who have good experiences and positive relationships have a better chance of achieving a satisfactory adjustment.

> Jamal, an adolescent boy aged 16, fled from Iran after the murder of many of his relatives. He was not sure if any of his family had survived. He was placed in a foster family with whom he developed a close relationship. He felt supported by them and was able to make good use of his educational opportunities.

How a child settles down and progresses educationally depends to a large degree on whether their school experiences are generally positive or negative.

> Two boys had quite different outcomes although their situations were similar. Both had lost their mothers and were finding it upsetting to have new step-mothers, and both had difficulties learning English. They were both showing aggressive behaviour in school, but one was suspended and the other was involved in a homework club for refugees. There he received extra help with English as well as support from the group. The suspended boy continued to have difficulties in school, whereas the supported boy began to make progress and become more settled.

Failure at school for whatever reason is also likely to produce secondary difficulties in behaviour, and perhaps lead to dropping out and hopelessness.

❏ LOSS and CHANGE OF CARERS

When flight leads to a change of carer, children's grief might go unnoticed. If the new carer is the child's mother it is unlikely that anyone will be concerned about this change of carer even if they are aware of it.

> Phu was brought up by his grandmother in Vietnam from the age of 7, his mother having fled with her younger son. After his grandmother's death he was reunited with his mother at the age of 13. He found it difficult to deal with both the loss of his grandmother and resettling into a 'new' family and a new country.

> Libaan was carried from Somalia at the age of one year, with his mother and two siblings to escape the bombing. They lived together in a refugee camp in Ethiopia for a few months where conditions were appalling – little food or water, no medicine: sickness and death were common.

> His mother fled to Britain with the two older children and Libaan remained with his aunt in the camp. He was finally reunited with his mother four years later when he was 5 years old, but his aunt had to remain behind in the camp. He found it hard to settle down with these relatives who were 'strangers'. At

school he was easily upset and this led the other children to provoke him. When he responded aggressively he was blamed for fighting.

Fahdi, age 5, had been brought up by his paternal grandmother and his father because his mother became pregnant again soon after his birth and was unable to continue looking after him. After a horrendous journey his mother arrived in this country with Fahdi and three other young children. She was exhausted by his demands and by her efforts to comfort him.

At school he was usually quiet and withdrawn, making little progress in learning English. He missed his father and grandmother and every time the door bell rang he would run to see if it was them. He was sometimes aggressive at school and provocative at home.

Those who have lost close family, especially their main carer, or who arrive here as unaccompanied children without any adult to care for them, are most at risk of emotional upset. Separation from a child's main carer often sets up a train of secondary difficulties.

Ramala at age 12 was living with her sister who had two small children. The sister was only 22 years old and had little time for Ramala's concerns, her school work or lack of friends, and expected her to help care for the younger children. Ramala became extremely depressed and was always longing to be reunited with her mother. She stopped going to school and spent most of her time in bed brooding over her situation.

Other separations

Children who have close ties with absent grandparents, aunts and uncles, cousins, are distressed about these separations, particularly when their relatives are ill or in danger. They are especially upset if they had no chance to say goodbye: frequently there is no time or it is too dangerous for children to know they are leaving. In the turmoil of departure and settling into a new country there may be no time to deal with the feelings a child has about such separations.

BEREAVEMENT

Children's understanding of death evolves with age. At around four or five years they have some understanding of the meaning of death and by seven or eight the majority are clearly aware that it is permanent.

Young children may go on asking about where the dead person is. They may react with regressive behaviour such as wetting, losing their speech, behaving in a babyish way. They may stop playing and vary between withdrawn

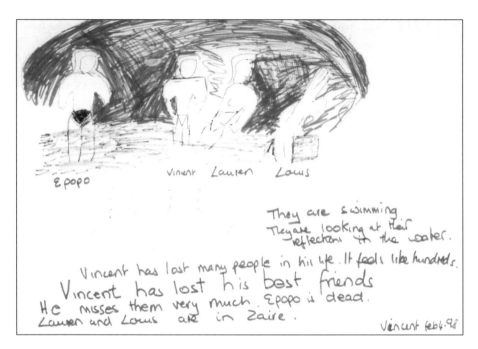

Epopo

Vincent Lauren Louis

They are swimming
They are looking at their
reflections in the water.

Vincent has lost many people in his life. It feels like hundreds.
Vincent has lost his best friends
He misses them very much. Epopo is dead.
Lauren and Louis are in Zaire.

Vincent feb4.98

Vincent has lost many people in his life. It feels like hundreds. He has lost his best friends: one is dead and two are in Zaire.

behaviour and wild excitable restlessness. They will be anxious about separations from familiar people.

Older children often feel different from their peers and want to be on their own. They may be angry and aggressive, or sad and clinging. Bedtime is often upsetting because children fear dreams about the dead person and because that is the time they need most comforting.

When there have been multiple losses and separations and the family has had to flee into exile, no-one has had time to mourn properly and the demands of daily life have to take precedence. The normal procedures of dealing with death cannot be observed and this hinders the process of mourning.

Children who have lost relatives through violence, especially if they witnessed the event, may find it difficult to mourn the death and come to terms with it. This is because the process of mourning is blocked by intrusive memories of the violence, which the child tries to suppress.

Family secrets and silences add to difficulties in dealing with distressing incidents when there is no-one to help the child to understand what has happened to them.

Adults have their own worries and may be preoccupied because it was impossible to hold a proper funeral, or because they were not able to be at the funeral. They may consider that the child is not affected by the loss and be irritated by their behaviour or too preoccupied to think about their needs. Children are helped by reassurance that they will be looked after and that however disrupted life has been, ordinary existence will continue. It is hard for parents to give this reassurance when they are worried about their asylum status.

School is important because it provides stability and normality, a place where it is legitimate to think about other things, achieve some successes, think about the future. Children can be helped by, for instance, providing the opportunity to talk if they want to, suggesting they write about how they feel (not necessarily to show anyone) or draw pictures about what has happened to them. Unfortunately many refugee children have no photos of their families, but some might want to make a memory book about their life before they became uprooted. Others find it comforting to writing a letter to the dead person, about all the things they would like to tell them.

Each member of the family may be mourning their losses separately and so be unable to give each other support. Some families are helped by meeting together to discuss their loss and through rituals begin the process of mourning (Parkes, Laungani and Young, 1997).

❑ TENSION AT HOME

Children usually sense their parent's tensions even if they do not know the cause, and are distressed by them. For example a mother may not tell her children that their father is dead or is not going to join them in exile, but they will be aware of her sadness about this. Even though parents try to protect their children by not discussing the atrocities or deaths that affect them, when parents are depressed or irritable or when their relationship is affected by their experiences, tension at home will affect the children.

Although children are living with parents or other relatives there may be no-one at home who can respond to their emotional needs and listen to their concerns (Melzak, 1995).

❑ CHILDREN AS CARERS

Even very young children are sensitive to the feelings of others and will attempt to comfort parents or siblings who are distressed.

> A boy aged 5 told his mother: 'Don't worry, it will be alright, I'll look after you.' He clearly felt he had to be the 'man of the house' now his father was dead.

Children try to cope with their own difficulties by themselves so as to protect their parents from further upset. They feel responsible for the family, often acting as the main carer in the family when the parents are distressed or preoccupied.

> Sonya, a 15 year old girl, took over the main responsibility for her two younger siblings because her mother was so distressed about her experiences of violence. Sonya also gave emotional support to her mother. At times she felt overburdened by all these responsibilities and this affected her studies.

❑ ILLNESS AND INJURY

Poor nutrition and sanitation in flight or in camps, and a dearth of medical care may have left children with untreated medical conditions. Many children have lacked medical care in their home country and some arrive with illnesses like malaria, TB, malnutrition, dental conditions, that need attention. Girls who have been raped are at risk of venereal infections and also of AIDS: there is then the sensitive issue of whether to carry out HIV testing. And it must be remembered that boys too are at risk of having been raped and will probably find it extremely painful to talk about it.

School nurses and community paediatricians have an important role in the health care of children. Not only in terms of identifying visual and hearing impairments, need for vaccinations and dental care, but also in identifying those at risk of emotional problems. Initiatives such as confidential drop-in clinics in school are easier to access than GP clinics and give a greater sense of confidentiality. They allow children to express anxieties about conditions such as menstrual problems and also worries over tensions at home or school work (J. Ellis, personal communication).

Children might be self-conscious about injuries which are a constant reminder of what they have been through and possibly provoke teasing.

> Emerico's finger had been deliberately chopped off and although not causing any real handicap he was still upset about it. His brother had a facial injury, as a result of an attack, and this was affecting him deeply. He refused to talk about his feelings, and was not making friends at school; he preferred to spend his time alone and was easily irritated.

Other children have chronic pain from scars or injuries which would benefit from treatment.

QUESTIONS FOR DISCUSSION

What are the main tensions facing refugee children?

What are the secondary adversities that children encounter? How could these be prevented?

Chapter 5

COMMUNITIES

❏ DIVERSITY

It cannot be assumed that all refugees from a particular country have undergone similar experiences or have the same attitudes and beliefs. They come from diverse cultures and backgrounds: rural and urban; rich and poor; affected by Western and by traditional influences to differing degrees; with varying religious and political backgrounds. They have arrived at different periods, and are at different stages of settlement. As there are differences within and between refugee communities, generalisations must be made cautiously, whilst recognising many common issues. It is necessary to clarify with refugees themselves what they have been through, what their difficulties are, and how they see their situation.

Refugee communities can be a crucial support for their compatriots. They provide advice and befriending and an informal network that is often the best source of information about housing, benefits, interpreting and translating services. Where there is a Community Centre this can serve as a meeting place for social and cultural life.

Many Community Centres are widely representative, others represent more limited groups. As mentioned, refugee communities are not homogenous but differ on important dimensions such as social class, political and religious affiliation, clan or ethnic group, and language. These differences can become accentuated as exiles strive to reaffirm their identity and cohesiveness within their group, and this can lead to tensions within communities (Eastmond, 1989).

❏ ISSUES OF TRUST

Refugees often come from countries where there is no free speech and an absence of justice; collaborators with the oppressive forces infiltrate religious or political groups; torture is used to make people denounce their colleagues; arbitrary violence creates a climate of fear and suspicion. These actions have the aim of destroying opposition, individuals' capacity to resist, and normal social compassion. Even private life becomes invaded by the tentacles of the State.

The social bonds that held the community together are fractured by the experiences of oppression and uprooting and are difficult to rebuild in an alien environment. Adults withdraw into themselves and it may take a long time before their distrust is overcome.

When they arrive here refugees may avoid their own compatriots because they do not trust them, and justifiably fear that agents have infiltrated their organisations. Political or religious disputes can be a cause of genuine risk either from government agents or from other refugee groups of differing beliefs. Thus in the UK there are representatives of different political parties who do not agree with one another, and distinct Muslim sects who keep themselves apart. Iranian refugees range from Monarchist supporters, to left wing groups, to ex-supporters of the current regime.

Others avoid their compatriots because they do not want to be reminded of their suffering in the country of origin. They do not want to dwell on all they have endured and often say they do not like being with compatriots because all they talk about is their misery and the terrible situation in their homeland. They prefer to be with people who talk about 'neutral' or positive things.

Rebuilding a sense of community and developing social bonds with the host community as well as with compatriots, are necessary steps towards well-being. However some individuals or families do remain quite isolated because they feel it is better not to mix. In these cases the possibility of making contacts with other refugees and the host society are particularly important.

Communities change over time as refugees become more integrated and realise that return to the home country is not possible in the foreseeable future. They may lose some of the cohesion and take on some of the values of the host culture, especially the younger people who have grown up in the new environment (Eastmond, 1989).

QUESTIONS FOR DISCUSSION

How are communities affected by exile?

How could you promote links between refugees and host communities?

Chapter 6

WHO AM I?
ISSUES AROUND IDENTITY

Becoming a refugee presents both adults and children with questions about who they are and where they belong, because they have lost the surety of their place in the world. This uncertainty may be compounded by a sense of meaninglessness in their situation. They struggle to make sense of what has happened to them, to link outer reality with their inner feelings of loss and fear. Those with strong political or religious beliefs are often sustained by a framework in which to place their experiences (Eastmond, 1989).

The loss of the familiar culture with all its richness of customs, rituals and relationships has been likened to cultural bereavement. Nostalgia and long-ing for the past are mingled with bitter memories of the betrayal and injustice that led to uprooting (Eisenbruch, 1991, Loizos, 1981, Munoz, 1980).

When they arrive here migrants must construct anew their sense of where they belong. It is hard for us to realise just how insecure some children in this situation feel, and how much they need to cling to any kind of security how-ever temporary.

> Amir arrived at age 12 as an unaccompanied child from Iran and was placed in a detention centre for two days while a more appropriate place was sought for him. When the social worker came to collect him he did not want to leave but wished to stay in the centre which he already saw as a place of refuge.

> Patoo arrived as an unaccompanied 9 year old. He was admitted to hospital soon after arrival and stayed for a few weeks. At one point the ward staff wanted to change the position of his bed, but he became so distressed by this move that they had to leave him where he was.

It is common for adult refugees to emphasise their religious or political beliefs or their cultural practices, so as to sustain their identity. This means that parents become stricter about religious observance, more concerned about political distinctions, than before.

❑ INTEGRATION

Refugees arrive with varying ideas about their future. At one extreme are those who think it will be impossible to return to their country of origin, because of the political situation or because they have suffered so much there. They want to construct a new life for themselves as best they can.

At the other extreme are those who want to return home as soon as possible and do not wish to become integrated into the host society. They see their situation as temporary, and this makes it very difficult for them to adapt to the new country or begin to learn a new language (Eastmond, 1989). This is in contrast to emigrants who have chosen to leave their country of origin and definitely intend to stay.

Adjustment depends partly on age. Older people often want to maintain their previous way of life as much as they can and may remain detached from the host culture. Children do not have this choice because attendance at school and college inevitably forces them into close contact with the host society's values and customs, and the culture of their peers.

A satisfactory integration is a complex process, in which there is a constant evaluation of past experiences, coming to terms with the life that is lost, and re-evaluating the life that is new (Hoffman, 1996). Important influences on integration include aspects of the host society, the family, and the child's own attitudes to identity and integration (Finlay and Reynolds, 1987).

❑ INFLUENCE OF THE HOST ENVIRONMENT

As described in Chapter 2 a major source of distress for many refugees is the difficulty in gaining refugee status. After expecting safety and asylum they are shocked when they are not believed. An important influence on migrant's adjustment is the discrepancy between their hopes on arrival in the host country and the gradual realisation that their ambitions are not going to materialise (Littlewood and Lipsedge, 1989). Many refugees are disheartened by the racism and discrimination they meet, and by encountering people who believe that their asylum claims are not genuine.

Continuing barriers such as unemployment, limited English, and unresolved asylum status can result in years of feeling unsettled. This unease may even increase over time. In a study of 150 Vietnamese young people aged between 14 and 24 and their carers, symptoms of anxiety and depression rose over time in both groups, with carers showing the highest rates (Liebkind, 1983).

❑ GENERATIONAL DIFFERENCES

Usually responses to integration are complex and change over time. Adults often differ from their children: they already have a strong identity whereas young people are in the process of development and often ambivalent in their attitudes. They may feel guilty about losing interest in their original country or not feeling identified with the struggles going on at home. Because of what they went through there they may reject parent's accounts about the positive aspects of their home country.

> A Bosnian youth told me he felt guilty that he was not fighting to defend his own country and that he wondered whether he would ever be able to go back because of this.

> Another boy, aged 14, said he never wanted to return to Bosnia because of the horrors he had endured there, but that he knew his parents would want to go back if they could and he did not want to let them down.

For other young people the urgency to return conflicts with the wish to take back something useful.

> Jahal, aged 13, did not want to give up his identity as a Somali but was not sure how he could combine studying and doing well at school with his strong identification with Somali culture.

Parents are also often ambivalent and give mixed messages to the children about assimilating the values and behaviour of the host culture. They encourage ambition and hard work at school and at the same time criticise

My house in Bagdad. We had to leave.

many aspects of the way of life in the West. They worry about dangers and temptations in the West, and are unwilling to promote integration or let the children go out of the house. They fear that children will adopt the values of the host country and that this will lead to disruption of the family and loss of respect for adults.

Parents do not always understand the value of promoting children's knowledge about their own country, and maintaining language and culture. Some refugee children grow up knowing little about their country of origin or about the political struggles that led to their uprooting. Identity, a sense of belonging to a particular group, of knowing who one is, having an established place in the world, is a basic foundation for confidence and self-esteem. For many people it is linked to a historical sense of continuity, to links with past generations and the land where they lived. Continuity is often maintained through detailed knowledge about kinships and genealogies, and through rituals and ceremonies (Lewis, 1994). Uprooting disrupts this sense of continuity: it is particularly disturbing when it is not possible to bury relatives in the usual place using the customary ceremonies, or even to be present at the funeral.

Issues about identity and loyalty are particularly salient for adolescents. Hoffman describes in her book *Lost in Translation* how she had to adapt at the age of thirteen years when her family immigrated to Canada from Poland. She needed to understand her new culture as well as maintaining bonds with the old, and was concerned about 'the ...dangers of both forgetfulness and clinging to the past'. She felt 'stuck in time' and only after learning English properly, developing friendships, and becoming attached to the new country could she begin to move forward. She recounts how she did not want to become assimilated into Canadian society, that is to lose her old culture which she still valued, but to become integrated so that past and future would each contribute to her identity. This process of developing a 'bicultural' identity can be particularly complex for children who have to deal with both growing up and growing into a new society.

The development of a 'bicultural' identity, valuing aspects of both the past and the present, facilitates social bonds with compatriots and host society. This is a process that will take many years, and both parents and children have to accept that there will inevitably be differences between them in how they respond to exile.

A profound dilemma arises for those who are ambivalent about returning to their home country, or who are unsure whether they will be allowed, or forced, to return. Each person's decisions are contingent on many factors:

possibilities of return, incentives to stay or go back, phase of life, political considerations, family influences, experiences before and since exile.

Possibilities of integration also depend on the attitudes of people in Britain, and whether they respect the migrants and their culture. Migrants cut off by language and cultural barriers and unfriendly neighbours are isolated and have little chance to learn about Britain.

The development of a bicultural identity can be helped in school by supporting the child's involvement in their culture through

- encouraging first language classes, and taking GCSE in the first language

- encouraging children to talk and write about their country in the first language as well as in English, if necessary translating the texts into English

- inviting adults from the refugee community to visit school and talk about their life

- class discussions about different countries linked to the National Curriculum eg history, geography, literature including oral and written traditions

- creative activities linked to the refugee experience or to different cultures (see Chapter 12)

- promoting links with supplementary schools

- helping community centres to develop cultural activities for young people

❏ USING LANGUAGE AT SCHOOL AND AT HOME

Language is an important element in maintaining cultural identity. That is why oppressive governments often forbid the use of minority languages or education. Because of prohibitions about using their language, many children living in Turkey were not able to learn Kurdish and only speak Turkish.

Most children manage to learn English and maintain their mother-tongue – but not all. Children who are learning English at school begin to use English at home amongst themselves, and can start to feel that as the majority language it is more important. Younger children or those born in this country might lack fluency in their own language and never learn to read and write it. Communication between parents and children is affected when the adults are not learning English and the children are using the mother-tongue less and less. Family members can differ markedly in their language use depending on their experiences.

A Vietnamese mother who had been in Britain for four years had learnt very little English; as she had no strong links with the Vietnamese community she was

> quite isolated. Her son age 11 had been in school since he was 7; he spoke good English and had English friends. His spoken Vietnamese was reasonable but he could not read or write it.

> The second child, a girl of 13, had been in the country for about eighteen months following family reunion. She was making little progress in English, and felt isolated and miserable. Her reading and writing in Vietnamese were good, but she was not practising these skills.

Supplementary schools, in which reading and writing in the first language are taught, are very important in maintaining first language literacy. This does not interfere with acquiring English. Contrary to what one might expect, research (among others Cummins, 1984 and Edwards, 1998) shows that developing first language skills and doing some school work in their own language promotes overall capacities to think and learn. This is related to the ease with which complex ideas and new concepts can be developed in the first language.

Some children are not motivated to keep up or learn skills in their own language. They resent having to spend extra time in supplementary school especially if the lessons are rather formal, but it is important to encourage first language learning.

❑ GENERATIONAL CONFLICTS

Friction is likely when the process of adaptation affects the generations differently: usually children model themselves on their peers and take on more of the values and customs of the host society than the parents. They are more likely to become integrated than adults, especially if they were young when they migrated. Children may well come to know more about the host country than their parents and become critical of their lack of 'know-how'.

The freedom enjoyed by British young people is not acceptable to most adult refugees. They fear that if their own children have the same freedom they face serious risks, such as pregnancy, drug addiction and crime. Anxiety to protect their children makes them much stricter than they were in the home country. They also fear that children will lose their sense of family and abandon their parents in old age.

> A teenage boy did not come straight home from school as he was meant to, but hung round the streets with his friends for an hour or so. This led to increasing friction with the father who formerly had expected his son to come home early and to obey without question, He was unable to accept his son's behaviour and arguments were frequent.

Leila, also a teenager, came from a Muslim family. She wanted to wear short skirts, stay out later, and have boyfriends like her mates. This behaviour was quite unacceptable to her mother, who felt she had to be extra strict because she had no husband there to back her up.

Girls in particular find themselves in difficulties because traditionally they have led more restricted lives: they have stayed at home helping their mothers whilst boys have been allowed to move more freely. Parents may put pressure on girls to leave school and go to work or to have an early arranged marriage (Nguyen and Williams, 1989). When the honour of the family is linked to the good behaviour of the daughters, any girl who does not conform puts this honour at risk. Style of dress, using make up, staying out beyond their 'curfew' time causes anxiety to parents. A girl who is seen talking to a boy gives rise to gossip and worries about her reputation.

It can be difficult for parents and children to compromise in these situations. Parents cannot know what it is like for a child to live between two cultures, and children do not always sympathise with the parent's views; they want to fit in with their peers and do not want to be ostracised or laughed at. Sometimes young people leave home because they cannot accept parental rules, or because they are punished harshly for their behaviour.

Possible ways of dealing with intergenerational conflicts are:

- enlisting the aid of a respected person from the community to talk to parents and child. This may not work out if the elder supports the parental view and does not work towards any kind of compromise with the young person.

- parent group or individual discussions on generational differences, methods of discipline, and rearing children in a new culture

- discussion groups for young people on changing views in generations

QUESTIONS FOR DISCUSSION

How would you describe yourself? What helped to form your identity?

What could you do to help refugee children develop a positive bicultural identity?

What are the particular difficulties faced by girls in refugee communities?

How can community centres help children's development?

SECTION 2
HELPING CHILDREN AND FAMILIES

Chapter 7

COMMUNICATION AND UNDERSTANDING

❏ THE IMPORTANCE OF COMMUNICATION

Communicating is not just about learning another language or finding a good interpreter. It is also about understanding cultural norms and how others see the world. It is about acknowledging and accepting differences in ways of life, expressing feelings, dealing with distress, and bringing up children. Good communication depends on being curious, interested in other people and their differences, in spite of the effort required, especially when there are so many different ethnic groups.

Even though refugees come from such vastly different backgrounds there are a number of common themes that frustrate understanding between host and refugee communities. In particular Western ideas about the family, including individuation and independence, the importance of the nuclear family, and an emphasis on competition and achievement, diverge from those in Asian and other Eastern cultures. These latter emphasise obligations towards the family, cooperation and striving for harmony with others.

Cultural sensitivity commonly means being sensitive to the norms of other, usually minority, cultures. But it should also include awareness of one's own culture, beliefs, attitudes, practices, and how these create preconceptions about other cultures and affect the way we behave to others.

❏ LACK OF TRUST

Refugee families usually come from oppressive societies that forbid criticism of government or protest at injustice: no one knows who is a collaborator, who is a potential betrayer. As a safety measure parents may impress upon their children that they must not tell anybody *anything* about themselves (Melzak, 1992).

They may have lived through situations where it was dangerous to show any emotion when faced with terrible sights because those who did risked punishment. Even after reaching the host country they still fear that information might get back to government in their own country and perhaps have repercussions on their relatives there.

All this makes it difficult for many refugees to trust others easily. Children may have lost faith in adults who could not protect them or who commit atrocities, and may be wary of making friends with other young people.

> Nicole, who was living with an uncle because her parents were both dead, was told not to divulge this to anyone in case it affected her asylum status. This secrecy prevented her from dealing with the deaths of her parents for whom she was still mourning.

Because of secrecy and distrust some refugees only trust someone from their own community. On the other hand they may prefer to seek help from outside their own community so that they do not have to worry about confidentiality. For example, adolescent girls rebelling against the strictures of their families may prefer to have a social worker from outside their community. This is because they think that a social worker from their community will be totally identified with the parents' values, will not respect their point of view, and may not preserve confidentiality.

Both adults and children need time to feel safe, to be sure that others understand their situation and can be trusted. Even if they have persistent worries or concerns they may choose not to talk about any personal matters.

Secrecy and uncertainty

In many cultures it is not the custom to tell children about death or other bad news until they are 'old enough to understand'. The age at which children are considered able to understand and deal with this kind of information can vary between around eight years to late teenage years.

It is especially difficult to explain to a child the fact that someone has 'disappeared', ie been taken away by the military or police, and that no-one knows whether they are alive or dead. Children may hope for many years in vain that a loved one will return. Often children suspect that someone has died or is not able to join the family in this country, and their uncertainty and anxiety give rise to behavioural and emotional difficulties.

In these cases knowing the truth might help them. It is essential to discuss this issue thoroughly with parents and respect their point of view. Unfortunately sensitive information is sometimes given to children by professionals without discussing this properly with the parents. Relatives or guardians should decide when it is best to tell the child, and preferably the information should be divulged by them.

Relations with authority

Refugees may lack experience of the kind of state and welfare services that exist here and find it hard to understand their entitlements or the functions of various professionals. They probably have not come across social workers before and have no concept of their role. When they have come from circumstances of oppression and violence they usually mistrust authority and officials. Apparently innocent questions may be seen as dangerous, lest sensitive information be passed to the Home Office or even to representatives of their home country. The difficulty of claiming asylum increases anxiety.

This lack of trust is reinforced by what is viewed as arbitrary interference in their lives by officials. Social Services Departments are seen as particularly threatening because of the way they take children into care on what seem to the refugee communities to be unreasonable grounds.

❏ FAMILY TIES AND INDIVIDUALISM

Refugee families usually come from societies where life is based around the extended family, which provides a kinship network of relationships, mutual responsibilities and obligations. The extended family is much wider than is now the custom in the West, and cousins, aunts and uncles, or even more distant relatives, play a more important role. Social obligations are given high priority (O'Brian, 1995, Dwivedi, 1995, Lau, 1995). This can be contrasted with the smaller family networks of the West and the emphasis on individuality and independence.

Instead of having a ready-made social network as before, refugees find they have to construct a new social life in an alien milieu. They are surprised by the more private lives that people lead here and that neighbours do not know each other.

Views of childhood

Childhood may be viewed rather differently in the host and refugee community, if in the latter children are expected, for example, to have responsibility from an early age and to help with work at home such as cooking or child care.

Children may be encouraged to respect their elders and to put the needs of the family first; there is no thought that one day the child ought to separate from the family. In contrast Western childhood is supposed to be a privileged time with no responsibility; independence is encouraged, with the goal of one day leaving home. The freedom of Western children, who usually have few responsibilities, come and go as they wish once in their teens, and generally run their own lives to a great extent, surprises many refugee parents who expect their children to have responsibilities for child care or helping in the home. We do not expect children to take on so many responsibilities and may even consider that children are being exploited when, according to themselves and their families, they are helping as expected.

❑ ATTITUDES TO COUNSELLING AND PSYCHOLOGY

In this century the West has become very 'psychologically minded'. As expectations of suffering have been reduced, and religion is rarely seen as a major source of consolation, we have needed to find a new framework that makes sense of affliction and this has taken the form of a psychological framework. Events which once were considered as 'normal' risks of life are seen as threatening and requiring some type of therapy: psychological treatment or counselling are now recommended for many causes of distress, eg following a difficult birth, illness, or an accident.

In addition rising standards of living and increased life expectancy have raised expectations of a fulfilled life amongst the better off. Therapies are often sought to release creative potential and heighten a sense of well-being.

Whereas at one time explanations of misfortune were based on religious frameworks, destiny or chance, it is now common to find someone to blame for bad luck, and this is reflected in rising levels of litigation. It has been suggested that coping strategies are diminished by these attitudes (Furedi, 1997).

In contrast many cultures of the world, facing harsh life circumstances and violence, have maintained a stoical approach to difficulties. They consider that lengthy 'talking through' of their problems is self-indulgent and counter-productive, and that they must endure their situation as best they can. In the West this attitude may be seen as denial, whereas from another viewpoint it could be seen as a good coping method under extreme difficulties.

Western-style psychological treatments are alien to refugees and are often thought to imply that they are 'mad'. They can draw upon other traditions of healing, ritual and ceremony for dealing with adversity, for example traditional healers (Loncarovic, 1996, Tang, 1994), although these may be unavailable to those in exile. Counselling is not always acceptable. Refugees are often more interested in practical solutions to their problems, and earning money and becoming independent is seen as the best way of improving well-being. They expect to be given advice about their difficulties, as this would be offered in their own culture, and non-directive counselling seems remote and unproductive.

Offers of support must take into account the beliefs and attitudes of recipients and be made in a framework that is acceptable and meaningful to them. Ideas that children should be autonomous and that independence from the family is the desirable aim for a mature adult are based on Western notions, and are discordant with many non-Western concepts. Similarly, the techniques in family therapy of encouraging children to talk about their parents in front of the therapist violates rules of respect and appropriate communication in cultures where rules of discourse are more formal and in-depth exploration of feelings are not customary.

Various organisation are attempting to develop therapies that are acceptable to different cultural groups. They are also promoting the training of people from different ethnic minorities who can provide relevant support that is culturally meaningful (see Nafsiyat, Appendix).

❏ THINKING ABOUT BLOCKS TO COMMUNICATION

It is understandable that difficulties can arise when people from different cultures try to communicate.

Possible causes of difficulties in communication with an adult refugee are:

- practical problems with understanding the language or with interpreting
- not trusting the interpreter
- issues are too painful to talk about
- time needed to develop trust
- fears of not being understood or accepted
- fears that confidentiality will not be maintained
- misunderstandings about the content of the conversation, finding questions intrusive

Trusting others can be particularly difficult for those who have been tortured. An Iraqi man who had been tortured and whose wife had been killed was so suspicious that he would not agree to having an Iraqi interpreter even though his English was very limited.

Communicating with parents

Communicating with parents requires the development of trust, using good interpreters when required, and initially indicating that any problems that do arise can be discussed without blame.

If the parents are already familiar with the school, communication will be easier when problems do arise.

Communicating with children

Communication with refugee children may be difficult because

- they are confused about what has happened in the past, especially about the details and chronology of their lives. Especially if they are young they may have misunderstood what happened to them or what they witnessed

- they have been told by parents not to talk to others

- they want to please the person talking to them and say what they think that person wants to hear

- some topics are too upsetting to talk about

- they are afraid of repercussions, and are not sure who they are talking to or what use will be made of the information

- they are afraid of stigma (Richman, 1993)

Some children display no problems but have been told by parents not to discuss their situation with anyone. These children may not know why they were sent here and are not necessarily traumatised but believe that they must just get on with their education, as this is what their parents will expect. Their silence may be surprising to teachers or others who expect children to talk about themselves.

Some suggestions for improving communication with children are:

- ensuring regular contact with the child

- showing that you understand their reasons for distrust

- giving practical advice and information where possible

- having a good interpreter

- finding activities that you can enjoy together

- communicating through non-verbal activities like art and mime (see Chapter 12 and Richman, 1993)

- learning about the history and culture of their country

- getting to know the parents – if they are here

Good communication by helpers can be blocked in situations where:

- there is no common language and no interpreter, or the helper imagines that the other person understands more English than he or she does. It is common for mistakes to be made about how much English is understood. It is important to check by asking people to repeat what you have said; merely asking if they have understood can be misleading as we all have a tendency to say 'yes' in this situation

- the helper becomes upset or overwhelmed when faced with the refugee's difficulties. Other strong emotions such as anger, irritation or distrust can also arise when faced with stories of atrocities and misfortune

- the helper cannot understand other cultures or other points of view. For example a teacher would not accept that Muslim girls could not do gym during Ramadan because they were fasting all day. Some social workers cannot accept that parents do not inform their children about the deaths of relatives, forgetting that only very recently has this been advised in this country

- preconceptions block free communication eg being afraid to ask straightforward questions because all refugees are thought to be traumatised

- not respecting refugees. For instance, one housing officer tried to rush a refugee mother into taking a flat she was offered although her health would have made it very difficult for her to climb the stairs up to it.

- the helper does not create trust, or realise the importance of confidentiality

- work with refugees is not valued in the organisation and pressure of time makes contacts too hurried; or if the risk of burn-out is high

QUESTIONS FOR DISCUSSION

Communication and understanding

What preventive measures could promote mutual understanding between the receiving and refugee communities?

What do you think you need to explain to a refugee family about life in Britain? What would you think it was important to discuss with refugee parents about neighbours, how families function, and child rearing practices in this country?

A refugee mother arrives here from Iraq with one 5 year old. What do you think would surprise her about life here?

Blocks in communication

What are the causes of difficulties helpers have in communication? How could these difficulties be overcome?

A boy aged 17 is isolated and unwilling to talk about his past life. It is difficult to know what his past history has been and whether he needs extra support. What could be the cause(s) of his reticence?

How would you set about developing communication with a 9 year old Somali girl who has just come to this country and does not speak English?

Chapter 8

WORKING WITH INTERPRETERS

It must be remembered that refugee communities are not homogenous. There are political, religious, and ethnic differences between people coming from the same country. It happens at times that an interpreter who seems to come from the same refugee group is not acceptable or trusted because of these differences, for example between Bosnian Serbs and Muslims, various Somali clans, diverse political parties.

The gender of the interpreter is also relevant. Men may not be used to talking about themselves in front of a woman; women may be embarrassed to talk in front of a male interpreter, and if they have been raped they might feel extremely anxious.

When no interpreter is available it is customary to use whoever is at hand be it a child, relatives or a bilingual stranger. Although any of these might be acceptable when it is a question of imparting simple information, there are serious disadvantages for more personal matters. Confidentiality may not be protected, and the language skills of the interpreter may not be adequate.

Children are frequently asked to take on responsibilities as interpreters and act as the intermediaries between the family and officialdom; these responsibilities may be unsuitable, and could expose children to inappropriate knowledge. There is also the risk that adults will not talk freely about their health if a child is interpreting for them. Children may hear information that would normally have been hidden from them, and their role upsets the customary relationships within the family. At times they miss a great deal of school because of the demands on their time. They may become confused if they see that what refugees say is not believed by those who are talking to them.

An interpreter must have the trust of the people they are interpreting for and it is essential to discuss beforehand any tensions that may arise between interpreter and refugee. The possibility of incompatible beliefs always needs to be checked out first. Do not be hesitant about asking about whether a proposed interpreter is acceptable; the question will show that you are aware of the importance of this issue. Fortunately there are many people who are able to establish an independent, neutral role, and be accepted by diverse groups within a community (Shackman, 1995).

Interpreters must be able to deal sensitively with painful issues such as torture, rape, atrocities, betrayal, death. If they too have suffered from violence and oppression they may be more sensitive to someone else's feelings, or on the other hand they might find it harder to deal with certain topics.

The difficulties that can arise when working with interpreters, related to language and communication skills as well as emotions, are likely to be magnified when an untrained person is interpreting. These difficulties include the possibility that the interpreter

- belongs to a group who is not trusted

- is unsympathetic to the refugee

- does not speak English or the refugee's language well: often their English is limited or they are interpreting from a language that is not their own mother-tongue

- finds it difficult to translate certain concepts or emotional states from one language to another; it takes a refined understanding of both languages to do this, and the interpreter may not know the required terms

- lacks communication skills so translates insensitively or unclearly,

- lacks training so does not translate correctly in either direction: makes up answers, says what they think the other person ought to say, only repeats a very small part of what the client or helper has said. This can be obvious when you compare the length of the interpreter's speech with that of the client or helper.

- becomes upset by the conversation

- has conflicting loyalties and does not divulge certain things they have been told by the clients or already know about them, because this would betray their trust.

A poor interpreter will produce misunderstandings and frustration, and this leads to wasted time and energy. Certain procedures can, however, help the interviewer to make the situation more satisfactory to everyone concerned. For example, the interviewer should:

- ensure that the interpreter is acceptable

- stress the issue of confidentiality with the interpreter

- prepare themselves and the interpreter beforehand, discuss any ideas or concepts that might be difficult to translate, or any emotional difficulties that may arise

- speak clearly and simply; allow time for translating

- allow time for making introductions and establishing trust

- show respect for both the interpreter and the refugee

- allow time at the end to discuss any issues that have arisen in the interview, such as problems with interpreting or emotional reactions to an upsetting interview.

Good preparation and an awareness of the possible difficulties are necessary in order to work smoothly with an interpreter. Ideally, one would work with a familiar interpreter who has been properly selected, well trained in how to communicate with children and parents, and well supervised (Shackman 1995).

A good interpreter will be able to gain the trust of the family and clarify cultural issues for both the refugee and the helper. In practice there are difficulties in obtaining interpreters easily for all the different languages needed. It requires particularly good communication skills to translate for children.

QUESTIONS FOR DISCUSSION

Interpreting

What provisions exist for interpreters? Are they adequate?

How could you ensure that your requirements for good interpreters are met?

What are the difficulties of working with interpreters? How can you deal with this?

Chapter 9

WAYS OF HELPING REFUGEE CHILDREN and FAMILIES

Diagram 1 summarises the wide range of interacting factors, both past and current, that affect refugee children's well-being.

Diagram 1

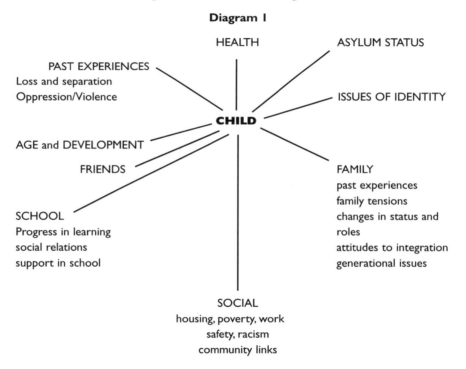

In spite of their histories of adversity most refugee children are able to deal with their experiences, providing they are living in an environment that encourages their development. A normal life with supportive adults and children, and hopes for the future, provide such an environment.

❏ SOURCES OF SUPPORT

The supportive factors that help children and that make life 'normal' for them include:

Having a family or other permanent carers that provide adequate care and affection

Mixing with adults and children who are friendly and understanding, and can be trusted

Education that meets their needs

Opportunities to play and work

Activities that promote self-esteem.

It is factors like these that help refugees to feel safe. Everyone who comes into contact with refugee children and their families, can help them by contributing to this supportive, normal environment. The role of 'ordinary' everyday contacts is crucial: if refugees meet with hostility or lack of understanding, these added stressors interfere with coming to terms with past difficulties and building a future.

Most refugees do not need specialist help. It is often assumed that all refugee children are 'traumatised' by their experiences and need specialist treatment, but in practice few refugee children require specialist treatment, and distress can often be relieved without recourse to specialists. Children often find it easier than adults to adapt .

The concept of being traumatised implies that a child (or adult) is imprisoned by overwhelming experiences in the past and cannot forget certain horrifying events, such as seeing someone killed, or suffering violence themselves. When these experiences have not been mentally 'processed' and dealt with adequately they continue to weigh on the mind and this is expressed through

- memories of the events that flash back into the mind like a film and produce emotions of panic similar to the initial experience
- feeling upset by reminders of past events such as men in uniform, aeroplanes, loud noises, or anything that reminds the person of previous frightening experiences, and trying to avoid these reminders
- poor sleep, nightmares about frightening experiences
- poor concentration
- exhaustion, aches and pains
- feeling different from others

Children are upset by other things besides these specific disturbing events in the past – separation from loved ones, loss of all they held dear. They are also troubled by current stressors – difficulties in learning or in social relations at school, cramped accommodation, worries about the future, domestic violence. These other sources of upset are often very distressing, especially loss and separation from loved ones, and problems over gaining asylum. Support has to take into account both past and present troubles; assumptions that events in the past are more upsetting than present experiences may lead us to ignore decisive factors in distress that now prevail, especially when refugees have to cope with long term difficulties, and the stressors they face are chronic and have no easy solutions (Richman, 1993, Gorst-Unsworth and Goldenberg, 1998).

❏ RESILIENCE AND COPING

Like adults, children vary in how they deal with adversity.

Helpful factors in the past that promote coping in the present include

> a stable and loving family
>
> strong moral, religious or political beliefs imparted by their family, that can continue to guide and support the child

Current factors that help them include

> supportive parents or other carers who are coping well with their situation
>
> information about their situation that helps them to make sense of what has happened to them
>
> having someone to confide in
>
> the capacity to seek help from others
>
> the capacity to use different ways of dealing with problems
>
> sharing experiences with others in a similar situation
>
> friends
>
> moral support in school
>
> progress in school work and English, and other successes
>
> being encouraged to have a positive attitude to their own culture and language
>
> Having an interest or activity that they enjoy pursuing
>
> Hope for the future – expectations that their future will be satisfying and secure.

Those who are flexible in the ways they cope with difficulties are more likely to manage in times of stress. Different ways of coping include:

- being able to mobilise help from others

- talking things over with friends

- taking practical steps to solve problems when this is possible.

When no practical steps are possible ways can be sought to feel better such as:

- thinking about good times in the past or the future

- not dwelling on an insoluble problem

- finding ways of distracting themselves, for example through sport, music or other activities, or meeting with friends.

It seems that skills in coping with adversity are partly learnt through family guidance and styles of coping, and partly related to a child's temperament.

> Hamid, an unaccompanied 17 year old, was living in a foster home and was giving rise to concern because he was isolated and irritable. He spent a lot of time in his own room and was not making friends or achieving well in college. When asked about his difficulties he always said he wanted to manage on his own and refused help.

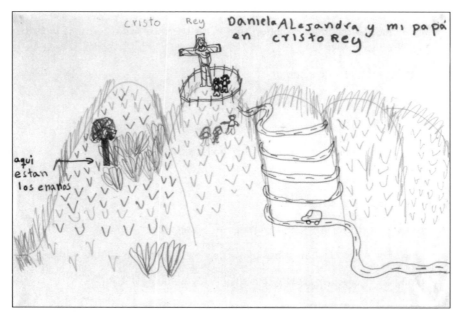

Remembering a happy time with my father

This boy had many changes of carer before he arrived in this country and had led an unsettled life. It seemed that he had not developed ways of dealing with the difficult situation he was now in; he could not accept help from others and found it difficult to trust people.

In contrast Ernest, an unaccompanied 16 year old, was in his own flat. He was doing well in college and had made some friends even though he was sad about his separation from his family. He came from a stable family and although he did not know whether his parents were still alive he was able to think of them as still guiding him: he thought about what they might have wanted him to do, and tried to fulfil their expectations of him.

Children's sense of security and self-esteem before they are exposed to adversity are vital factors in how they cope. For children of all ages it is the absence of their main carers that upsets them most (Sack *et al*, 1986).

❑ THE INFLUENCE OF AGE

Preschool children

Young children are particularly sensitive to their immediate family situation and to the loss of their main carer. Their distress is shown by withdrawal and their lack of interest in play or food; they may stop speaking and start wetting the bed, or have nightmares. At times they may be restless and overexcited or provocative.

Very young children are less aware of the implications of their situation and provided they have a caring family they will gradually begin to feel secure. However children soon reach the age of feeling the absence of their carers and then are likely to find it difficult to come to terms with their absence. It is particularly important for young children to have an adequate, stable family placement as soon as possible.

Young children may be particularly confused by school, particularly if they have not been to a kindergarten, and become quite wild and aggressive in this situation. They may react badly to separation, especially if they have ex-perienced previous separations and change of carers, and may need a while to get accustomed to being away from home and in a school setting.

Older children

As children get older they are more able to understand the situation of themselves and their families.

In school children become aware of being different, especially if they are mocked or bullied, and struggle to maintain their self-esteem and to learn.

Issues about identity and loyalty become more compelling, particularly for adolescents, as they plan for the future and consider their responsibilities for their family. Tensions between what the adolescent wants and the needs of the family can set up conflicts within the adolescent and between family members.

> A girl of 17, Olga, had taken on the major responsibility for looking after four younger brothers and sisters, because her mother was overwhelmed by her own problems and depressed. The eldest daughter continually thought about leaving home because of these responsibilities but felt that it was her duty to stay with the family.

Adolescents are particularly vulnerable because they are dealing with so many changes in their lives. They are at a stage of life when they should be moving towards adulthood but the social structure in which this would have happened has disappeared. It may feel as though they are living in a social vacuum, especially when parental guidance, advice and comfort are absent, because the social rules of the host society are so different. When they have no clear vision of what their future is going to be it is extremely hard to continue in education or to feel optimistic (Leibkind, 1983, Valtonen, 1994, van der Veer, 1992, 1993).

❑ A MODEL OF SUPPORT

Children and families are affected by events from the past, current stresses, and positive aspects in their lives. Support therefore needs to be multifaceted, to promote positive factors that can outweigh negative ones, building on the children's strengths, and giving them hope for the future (McCallin, 1992, Dagnino, 1992, Loncarevic, 1996).

Primarily the aim of support should be preventive, protecting children from secondary adversity, providing a normal life and a sense of security, promoting education and self-esteem, and supporting parents. This involves first providing basic services such as education, health, and housing and then ensuring that refugee children receive general support through school policies, recreation and creative activities. Relationships with teachers, other pupils and friends are especially important. The children need to be given opportunities to express themselves through group activities and discussions with people available for individual conversations, should they seek this. And they need support to their culture and that of their community, with language, literacy and religious teaching.

Support should start with this preventive approach as specialist services are required for only a minority. Moreover, offers of mental health services are viewed with suspicion and likely to be greeted with hostility as intrusive and unnecessary.

This does not mean that counselling, group work, individual therapy and family work should not be available but it means that they must be offered in an acceptable context (Reichelt and Sveaass, 1984). As an example, pre-school facilities can form a nucleus around which support groups for isolated mothers can grow, including English classes, advice on nutrition, stimulation and use of toy libraries.

QUESTIONS FOR DISCUSSION

What are the major factors causing distress in young refugee children, and in adolescents who are refugees?

What helps them to cope with adversity?

What should be provided as a basic system of support for children?

Chapter 10

I'M GOING TO SCHOOL!

Refugee children generally have high expectations of school and aspire to do well. Usually they want to learn, to be part of the new society, to 'belong' and have friends. They and their families see education as a way of surviving, making their way in the UK, developing skills to take home. However matters do not always run smoothly, and lack of English makes it difficult to sort things out (McDonald, 1995, Jones and Rutter, 1998).

Education is especially important for unaccompanied children; they feel it is an obligation to do well so that they can contribute to their family's welfare afterwards, or if they have no hope of reuniting with their family it helps them to have a positive attitude towards their future.

❏ UNFAMILIARITY WITH SCHOOL

Some refugee children have never been to school before – in Somalia school was disrupted for several years – or have attended a variety of schools inter-mittently. Those who have been to school in the home country are used to very strict discipline; they find the structure of the classroom and the behaviour of the other children in the West very disorderly, and complain about the lack of discipline. The style of teaching is problematic for them when it involves active learning rather than learning by rote.

Teachers realise that they may have to make allowances for children who are unfamiliar with school. For example children, especially younger ones, cannot always cope with the normal classroom setting and the routine of school; the novelty of school is fatiguing and their concentration span may be short. Because of all the practical burdens the family cannot organise their time, or the children go to bed late or sleep poorly and cannot get up in the morning (Beattie, 1994). For those having difficulties, teachers or ESL tutors find that flexible programmes, shorter lessons, and topics that are linked to practical activities and daily living skills are more productive (Beattie, 1994).

❑ PARENTAL INVOLVEMENT IN EDUCATION

In many countries parents do not expect to be involved in their children's education and are only called to the school when there is a serious problem. Once inside the school gates responsibility belongs to the teachers. There is a custom for Turkish parents to say to the teacher when they first bring the child to school: 'Here is my child, the flesh is yours, but the bones are mine'.

Parents find it hard to see how they can help their children, especially if they do not speak English and have little education. Yet parents can encourage learning even when they do not speak English.

> A Turkish 18 year old described how during their school years, her father had asked her and her brother every evening to report back on the day's study and homework tasks, even though he spoke very little English. She felt this was a crucial factor in her success at school.

Children feel unsupported when parents are not monitoring their school work and cannot communicate with teachers eg about career planning, bullying or other worries.

Parents who do not speak English are more likely to become involved when there is a school-home link worker who speaks the same language, or a teacher who works with the children in their own language. Holding meetings with parents in their own language about the education system and the school also promotes participation.

In the school systems of many of the refugees' home countries, children are in the class appropriate to their knowledge rather than linked to their chronological age. When a child in our system passes up every year, parents may be lulled into a false sense of security, and think that their children have no learning problems.

❑ INITIAL ASSESSMENT

Good initial assessments of children's potential and educational level, and decisions about how best to start them off in the education system, are basic to children's progress in school. But assessment is difficult, particularly of those who have never been to school before. Lack of trained bicultural workers or interpreters and deficiencies in available tests compound the difficulties, yet a good assessment and placement in the right class are essential.

Frequently it is difficult to know which class children should be in because of uncertainty about their age, eg a girl said to be eight years old was already passing through puberty and was obviously older. She was living with her sister who did not know her precise age. Such children are likely to find it difficult to make friends and may get teased. Sometimes carers do not know the exact age of the children or perhaps put their age as younger to ensure their access to schooling.

The practice of putting children in the class appropriate to their chronological age can be counterproductive and unnecessarily distressing. An extra year in a lower class in which a thorough grounding in English is obtained could save years of failure, distress, and need for extra input. This could be especially important when considering whether to place a child either in the first year of secondary school or the last year of primary school, or whether to give a child an extra year of nursery experience.

❑ LEARNING ENGLISH

Children lack opportunities to practice English if they have no English friends or have no-one at home who can help them. Many are not allowed out to play, which further restricts their contact with English speakers. The situation is more difficult in secondary school where they are faced both with learning a new language and a wide range of subjects with new material, especially daunting if they have never been to school before. Children who start their education in primary school are usually more confident in English.

> Juan, aged 13, arrived in this country with his aunt and two sisters, his uncle having arrived previously. His mother had been killed and his father disappeared. The family lived in cramped bed and breakfast accommodation but seemed to be settling in although they were all mourning the death of the mother. No-one at home spoke English.
>
> Juan was very eager to start school and make new friends. However once he started he did not progress as well as his 9 year old sister in learning English, and found the other boys less friendly than he had expected. He lost his cheerful disposition and became moody and irritable. At home he refused to practice reading and writing.

❑ RACISM AND BULLYING

Refugee children commonly report that they are treated in an unfriendly manner, teased or bullied when they arrive in school. They think this happens because they speak hardly any English or because of racism, and may get into trouble either for retaliating against those who tease or hit them, or by truanting. They tend not to tell their parents as they think this will not help, but feel safer if they are in a school where there are a number of children from their own ethnic group who can protect them.

A girl of 12 described how she was often pushed in the dinner queue, and when she pushed back she got blamed for starting trouble. On one occasion a plate of food was thrown on the floor and the other girls said that she had done it. As neither she nor her mother spoke English they were unable to put her side of the story.

Bullying causes children to stay away from school, to drop out, or to change school, and causes major disruptions in education as well as profound distress. Nineteen out of thirty three children who were interviewed described experiences of bullying and six of these had changed schools or were planning to do so (Richman, 1996).

QUESTIONS FOR DISCUSSION

What difficulties do refugee children face in school? How can they be alleviated?

How should bullying be prevented and dealt with?

Chapter 11

HOW SCHOOL HELPS

It is no exaggeration to say that refugee children's well-being depends to a major degree on their school experiences, successes and failures. Because they are unfamiliar with the education system and particularly when they do not speak English, parents cannot help their children as they would wish to, and children may be left to deal with difficulties alone.

School policies are a powerful tool for helping refugee children feel safe and normal again, and begin to learn. They can promote the child's confidence and integration, and prevent isolation and frustration. Failure in school can have a disastrous impact on children who are trying to reconstruct their lives and their self-esteem, and develop hope for the future. Educational progress and emotional well-being are mutually dependent.

Other books deal in greater detail with refugee education (Rutter, 1994, Jones and Rutter, 1998) and in this text the emphasis is on how school affects children's emotional well-being.

❏ SCHOOL POLICIES

Many schools are developing a variety of creative approaches which aim to support refugee children's learning and promote their self-esteem.

A school Development Plan as made by George Orwell school in Islington, London, gives a framework for these policies. They should be based on the following objectives:

- encouraging use of mother-tongue

- encouraging talking, including talking about home

- looking at loss, death and change in a safe way

- effective English teaching, involving all departments

- after-school clubs, especially for GCSE

- providing enjoyment, participation, collaboration, achievement and praise

- an antiracist and anti bullying policy

- tutors and Heads of year provide support

- regular monitoring of progress

- teaching about human rights and refugee issues in class

- staff training

- links with FE colleges to ensure student needs are met when they leave school

- links with communities (Wagner and Lodge, 1995).

Important aspects are good communication with parents and children, ensuring parent participation from the outset, having a good admissions and induction process, and health surveillance.

❑ GOOD COMMUNICATION

Good communication is the key to establishing trust, explaining how the school works and obtaining basic information about the child and family. This process is easiest when there is a home-school liaison worker or a teacher who speaks the family's language: failing this it is crucial to find an adequate interpreter. Sometimes an experienced parent can be helpful in explaining how the school runs: where sensitive material is involved this would not be suitable because of the issues of confidentiality and trust.

Good communication is also necessary for understanding the concerns of refugee children and their families, and trying to help them. Without this it is impossible to act in the child's best interests. Parents will not talk about important issues unless they feel safe.

An example of poor communication occurred when a Somali mother mistakenly thought her son's school was excluding him because he was aggressive and needed an assessment. In any case the mother did not want 4 year old Ali to go to school because he was threatened by the older brother of a child in his class, whom he had hit.

Neither his mother nor Ali spoke English so they could not communicate with either the teachers or the family who were threatening them as there was no interpreter available. The boy was off school for four months, during which time no action was taken.

He had been referred for assessment by his nursery school but because the family moved this was not followed through.

What families need to know about the school:

Parents need to know about the minutiae of school life which we take for granted, eg how subjects for study and exams are chosen, the organisation of the examination system, school expectations, routines, holidays, health checks, absences, play schemes, expected contacts with family, expected behaviour of children.

It is essential to translate letters and other information into the mother-tongue, so that even if parents cannot read they will be able to get it read to them.

Teachers need to know about the implications of routine measures. For example keeping children in after school is perturbing to parents who insist on children coming straight home from school. Some parents think that if their child is behaving badly in school there are no other possible measures but to expel him or her.

We may not realise how important information about ordinary life is for a stranger.

> One family were terrified when they heard loud bangs a few nights before November 5th. They though they were hearing gun fire and of course had never heard of Bonfire Night or Guy Fawkes.

Both parents and children need to know by name and sight one person in the school whom they can contact if they have concerns. Ideally the contact person would be a teacher, or school home link person, who speaks the same language as the parents.

❏ ENSURING PARENT PARTICIPATION FROM THE OUTSET

With good communication established it is possible to encourage parents to become involved in school life and their children's learning.

Schools suggest that the following actions are helpful:

- making sure they have an interpreter, working with parents from the start

- to have at least three meetings with parents in the first term as this is a crucial time for developing trust, for seeing whether the child is settling in and learning, and laying the foundation for the parents' participation. A good understanding of the child's past and present situation can be built up during this time

- organising meetings of parents from the same ethnic group with an interpreter or liaison worker, to discuss educational issues or other topics that are of interest.

- involving parents in various activities, eg

  to raise money for the school,

  to develop written material in their own language, such as books that the children can use

  working with children in their own language

  taking part in cultural activities

- organising English classes for parents at the school or a nearby FE college. Schools have found that this can be a useful way of forming a friendly network and strengthening the home school link, especially for women with young children.

There are many trained and able people in the refugee communities who are unable to find work. They are employed in some schools to act as liaison workers with parents, teach mother-tongue skills, give support in school work, and be a cultural interpreter for the school. They also act as role models for the children; for boys without fathers it is particularly valuable when the worker is a man.

Information for parents

Refugee mothers are often isolated and it is useful to know the kinds of support available locally so that parents can be informed about them or advised where they can obtain more information eg from health visitors.

Since they are unfamiliar with the school system and often have an interrupted or curtailed education, older children need careful careers guidance, and parents need to be involved in this process.

❏ HAVING A GOOD INDUCTION PROCESS

Teachers suggest the following steps:

- Getting to know the parent or guardian

- Introducing child and parents to school and explaining how school works, and the importance of parent involvement

- Ensuring that one or two children are designated to befriend the child, including if possible one child who speaks the same language

- identifying a contact person in school for child and parent

- a basic social and educational assessment

There are difficulties in deciding what to include in a basic social assessment, because teachers are reluctant to label children or to intrude too much. Camden has produced a health checklist with suggested areas to cover in an assessment, although its length makes it more suitable for a detailed assessment of a child with persistent problems (Camden Refugee Students Writing Group, 1995).

In school, children hope to be one of the crowd and get on with normal life and learning; neither they nor their teachers want them to be singled out as 'problem' children. On the other hand it is important to know something about the child's background so that preventive measures can be taken where necessary. An example was a child who was acting as a carer for his younger siblings because his mother was ill. The school was able to make allowances when the boy was occasionally absent or late for school, and to relieve him by initiating medical and social help for the mother.

The school can establish good communication from the start, through the induction process. Some of the issues to consider are:

> Whether parent, child, and school understand each other and whether there is an adequate interpreter when required

> What needs to be known about their culture, their past, their present, their expectations

A basic social assessment might include:

- who the child lives with
- details of moves and changes of carer
- whereabouts of the rest of the family
- asylum status
- housing situation
- vaccinations and health problems

A basic educational assessment might include:

- language(s) spoken at home
- child's previous education, achievements and language acquisition (Attainments in first language, and education (if the child already has some education) should be assessed with the aid of a bicultural worker.)
- child's current abilities in English
- parents' education, and knowledge of and literacy in English
- amount of educational support likely to be available at home

❏ PROMOTING ENGLISH AND MONITORING PROGRESS

There are many theories and opinions about how best to promote English language abilities amongst refugee children. At one time it was usual to withdraw children from class for extra lessons, then this was seen as making children feel different and was replaced by mainly giving help in the classroom. However there are now doubts about the efficacy of this latter approach and it is being queried whether an extended period of total immersion and continuing extra tuition might not be preferable.

Children with no English should not be deposited straight into a classroom without some preparatory language teaching. Although withdrawal of children from the classroom has became unpopular, some LEAs are now using withdrawal periods again to give extra language support, at least during the induction period and sometimes for longer.

Suggested actions include:

- regular homework

- English classes and regular monitoring of progress; experimenting with immersion teaching of English

- small group work and homework clubs to support English and homework. Often children have no space to do homework at home and no-one to discuss the work with.

Making a plan and reviewing

Depending on the initial assessment a plan of support can be made, which includes proper, regular reviews at not too long intervals so that a process of help can be initiated early on if it is required. Specific targets should be set so that it is clear whether or not a child is making progress at the expected pace.

It is recognised that some children pass through a silent period after arriving at school, until they feel safe and have settled in. However there is disagreement about how long this ought to be allowed to last before giving rise to concern, and before a detailed assessment is made.

Children's confidence increases over time as they feel less confused and more settled, but it seems a good rule of thumb to assess early rather than waiting to see how the situation turns out, in case a child has a serious disability such as a hearing impairment, learning difficulties, or emotional problems. If the reason for not progressing is thought to be due to the emotional effects of adversity in the past, this is all the more reason to expedite further assessment.

Some teachers consider that a year or even two years may be required before a child of normal ability starts speaking English. Others consider that if half a term or a term has passed and a child has shown no sign of speaking or making progress in learning there should be a thorough assessment. If children are not learning action must be taken quickly. According to some specialists in this field a good rule of thumb is that a silent period should not last for more than about six to eight weeks before action is taken.

It is essential to ensure that children are moving through language stages.

> A Turkish girl, Fatma, was hardly speaking English after two years in secondary school but just moved through the system. She was able to pass GCSE in Turkish, so demonstrating that she certainly had the capacity to progress in English. She thought her poor progress was related to bullying at school and to lack of more intensive English teaching.

More research is needed into the most effective ways of promoting English, and of assessing English competence (Jones and Rutter, 1998).

Refugee children are expected to learn from their age mates but many of them have little contact with native English pupils as they usually have to go straight home after school and never meet with English speakers outside school. Contact with other children promotes language but it has been pointed out that 'playground' English is colloquial and limited in content. There is a big leap between conversational English and the academic English required for passing exams.

Promoting first language

Maintaining first language skills and having some education in this language is advantageous for intellectual development (Edwards, 1998; Jones and Rutter, 1998). Starting off education in the child's first language promotes confidence and prevents feelings of anxiety when faced with an entirely new language.

If there is no teacher or home link person who speaks the child's language, it is useful to employ someone from the community who comes regularly to the school to give practice in first language literacy. Links with supplementary schools teaching in the first language can usefully connect the two educational experiences.

❑ ANTIRACIST AND ANTI-BULLYING POLICIES

Refugee children come from oppressive and violent situations and find it very painful when they are confronted with racism and bullying. It is disheartening to find that bullying is so common and that most children have given up hope that it can be dealt with. Aggressiveness is often a response to bullying which they cannot explain to teachers, and is the only outlet for the frustrations of not being able to explain in English what is happening.

There is increasing interest in using peer counselling as a way of supporting children at risk of bullying in schools (Tattum and Herber, 1993; Croall, 1995; Peer Counselling Networker, 1996).

❑ IMPROVING KNOWLEDGE ABOUT REFUGEE COMMUNITIES

For children and teachers actions might include:

- meetings in which members of the various communities talk about their history, life and culture, to teachers or groups of pupils

- group discussions and activities in the classroom (see section on activities)

- INSET training on bilingualism; curriculum issues; communication; discussing books and articles about the refugee experience or history

- cultural events involving parents and teachers

- using bilingual or other appropriate material (Rutter, 1991a, 1991b, Warner, 1991, Warner, 1995, Bolloten and Spafford, 1996)

- asking children to write about their experiences

- employing part-time workers from the refugee community as teachers or liaison workers.

❑ HEALTH SURVEILLANCE

Section 4 pointed out the health risks facing refugee children and the obstacles to health care caused by living in temporary accommodation and being highly mobile. It is particularly important to check on the children's health, hearing, vision, and dental and vaccination status in school since they may have missed out on these checks.

Some children have chronic pain following beatings or wounds which may require treatment.

It has been suggested that parent held health records for all homeless children would promote continuity in their health care and avoid going over the same ground every time they move.

QUESTIONS FOR DISCUSSION

What basic information do you think should be obtained about all refugee children?

How would you gain parent participation?

What would you consider to be the important elements of a school policy for refugees?

How would you run an induction process?

How could you promote English learning for refugee children?

Chapter 12

HOW ACTIVITIES HELP

Emphasis is placed on the importance of play for young children, as a means to explore the material world, develop social skills and promote creativity. Many refugee children have been denied these opportunities and have had little fun in their lives. Creative activities have a special relevance for all children who are deprived or who have special needs.

Benefits to refugee (and other) children of creative activities include:

- providing relaxation and enjoyment, and improving motivation to learn

- encouraging integration into a group

- developing social skills and friendships

- enabling success even if not good at English, raising self-esteem, and not overemphasising academic skills

- affirming a positive identity through activities related to children's culture

- exploring sensitive issues such as anger and bullying

- allow expression of feeling in a safe way

Many activities are non-verbal and enable children to express themselves without worrying about whether they are understood.

Teachers are using a variety of activities to promote the well-being of refugee children, increase their interest in learning, and raise awareness in others about refugee issues.

Many of these activities have been linked into various levels of the National Curriculum.

❑ TYPES OF ACTIVITY

Playground activities

Break time is often dreaded by children who fear bullying or rough games; if possible they try to stay indoors or help in the library during this time.

Anson Primary School in Brent has a high proportion of refugee children and many of the pupils live in temporary accommodation, so that school turnover is extremely high. They divided off the playground into different activity areas during break. One of the activities was organised by a play specialist who came to the school to teach circus skills to group of refugee and non-refugee children. In a few weeks they were impressing others with their juggling skills.

Sport

Success at sport does not depend on schooling or language; we know that involvement in a team has a great effect on children's self-esteem and involvement with others.

Oral history projects

Oral history projects can be integrated into the National Curriculum in a variety of ways, eg linked to history. Children learn about themselves and each other, and the value of different cultures, and discover that older people from different communities are a rich resource. *Talking Time* (Harris and Hewitt, 1991) is a good resource.

Oral history projects have proved very successful also with adult refugees in developing community cohesion and a sense of worth (Slim and Thompson, 1993). Oral history enables people to bear witness to their suffering and in this way to validate their experiences, and at the same time to feel more in control of their feelings.

Drama

Drama provides a means of helping children to explore different issues in a safe way. Refugees can work with others, using techniques such as tableaux, mime, basing an exercise on a theme or story. Children can participate in their own language and can be anonymous or risk exposing their vulner-ability as they wish (London Drama, see Appendix).

Theatre can lead others to think more deeply about refugee issues. The com-munity Theatre Group Leap used a play about refugees to stimulate dis-cussion with secondary pupils on the issues involved. They also developed a performance with a group of Kurdish young men, developing communica-tion through non-verbal means as well as through using Kurdish (see

Appendix). In another project at George Mitchell School video work on refugees was integrated into the Humanities National Curriculum.

Photos

Photos of their environment or history can be used to explore the history of immigrants or of individual lives, and could be part of an oral history project.

Music, singing and dance

Musical projects are an exciting way of integrating children. Most refugee communities have a rich musical tradition and children may be learning traditional instruments or music in their community centres.

Art

Art therapy is used by trained therapists as a way of helping children to explore their feelings and concerns. Even when not intended as a therapy art work is an important tool for children to express themselves, and can be used by a class or group to explore different cultures or themes such as war and loss, or future hopes.

Writing

Writing (in the first language, if preferred) stories, poems, letters, diaries, promotes literacy as well as helping children to gain mastery over their experiences. The bilingual books produced by the Minority Rights Group are an example of how writing gives value to past life and experiences (Warner, 1991, 1995).

Making books about their own country or writing traditional stories can be done with parents, and is an excellent means of involving them in the life of the school.

Gardening, nature

Refuge children talk longingly about how they miss the countryside, greenery, birds or the sea. Most come from a less urbanised environment and miss the freedom and beauty they knew. Studies of ecological issues, biology, geography, and especially gardening, are a link to these significant positive memories.

❏ GROUP WORK WITH CHILDREN

Creative activities with children provide an important preventive tool for integration and promoting confidence and self-esteem, and are extremely valuable for children with marked difficulties or when parents or children do not accept other forms of help.

Groups can be for children with a similar background or problem or based round an activity like art, gardening, or homework (Camden Language and Support Service Refugee Team, 1994). The group offers support and sharing of feelings, and non-threatening conversations about dealing with problems. Discussions about the painful issues of loss, disappointment, anger, identity and loyalty can be dealt with sometimes more easily than on an individual basis.

QUESTION FOR DISCUSSION

Are activities useful?

How do they help children? Where should they be done? In school, clubs, community centres?

What plans would you make for developing activities?

Chapter 13

ASSESSING REFUGEE CHILDREN

❏ BEHAVIOUR AND LEARNING INTERACT

Sadness, worries about asylum or the fate of relatives, painful memories, tensions at home, bullying, can all affect a child's concentration and ability to learn; they can also hinder motivation to go to school and to study.

Both the past and the present influence every child and often several factors are affecting them at once – the situation at home and school, the child's internal emotional state, learning difficulties. These interact together and have to be tackled at the same time. Children who have little English may be bullied and have difficulties in understanding the lessons; these factors in turn may make them irritable and aggressive. As with all children, the different aspects need to be considered together.

As mentioned already, when refugee children have gone through very difficult times it is easy to assume that all their difficulties are because they have been 'traumatised' by their past experiences. This can lead to paying insufficient attention to other aspects of their lives such as current tensions at home or lack of progress in learning English. The latter is very often overlooked and may well be the major problem the child faces, and the frustration caused may be the prime cause of subsequent behaviour difficulties.

Children are surprisingly adept at hiding their lack of English and may pass through years of school without this being recognised. They are ashamed to admit difficulties in learning and become depressed or disruptive, or truant from school.

❏ WHEN TO ASSESS

A basic social and educational assessment was discussed on page 69-70 and this should provide information which can be used for planning support in a child's first months.

In spite of good preventive policies and support in school, some children will require more attention because they are not learning or because of their behaviour at home or school. Early assessment of children with difficulties in behaviour or learning is important to ensure that the children make maximum use of their educational opportunities. Assessment and help for refugee children is similar to that for all children, even though it is sometimes complex because of the many aspects that have to be taken into account, and the obstacles to communication.

All assessments should end with a provisional formulation about the problem, a plan, and a decision about when to review progress and assess the need for a change of plan or more input.

A child who is making steady progress in learning, in understanding and speaking English and in mixing with other children and who does not show persistent behavioural or emotional difficulties that interfere with learning or relations with others, should not give rise to concern.

❑ HOW CHILDREN SHOW DISTRESS

What should alert us to the fact that a child might be in need of more help? Indicators include one or more of the following:

- the child is a slow learner in all areas or has some learning difficulties in English or in school work, so that child is not meeting the targets already established after the initial assessment on entry

- school attendance problems ie regularly missing school, truanting, or dropping out

- has social problems eg is in a class with children of a different age and finds this difficult

- is not receiving adequate care at home

- behaviour difficulties: aggressive, disobedient, disruptive

- has poor concentration, restless, overactive

- is isolated, does not have friends

- emotional difficulties: unhappy, anxious, fearful, poor sleep,

- a sudden change or increase in behaviour that signals distress, such as:

  an increase in confrontations;

  an abrupt withdrawal from others;

complaints of physical symptoms;

wetting or soiling;

inability to concentrate in class;

coming late, absences, truanting.

When difficulties are severe, persistent and multiple this indicates that further assessment is definitely required.

The possibility of bullying should always be considered since this may not be mentioned spontaneously.

There is no one to one relationship between symptoms of distress and causes of distress. For example aggression may be related to many factors such as confusion in school, frustration, bullying, past experiences of violence, domestic violence and abuse, bewilderment about their situation, anxiety about carers or about safety.

Assessment might be done in school by special needs and ESL teachers with the help of educational psychologists. More complicated cases may be assessed by child and family consultation services or specialised centres. Assessment might involve

- talking to parents and the child separately and together

- observing the child in class and playground

- appraisal of language abilities (English and mother-tongue)

- appraisal of learning potential and achievement.

❏ DELAYS IN ASSESSMENT AND SUPPORT

Early assessment and planning is important because it prevents problems from escalating and quite simple measures can often improve a situation. However procedures for accessing help for children in school are often delayed for a number of reasons.

Mobility

Frequent changes of housing disrupts children's learning and also delay mobilising help: the new school may not have details of a child's difficulties and any referral made in the original school cannot be followed through because of the long delay between referral and appointment.

Lack of information from the previous school or GP also prevents continuity. Because of high mobility amongst refugees, schools may assume that when a child does not come to school this is because they have moved. Education Welfare Officers may not be told that a child is absent and he or she may just drop out of education.

Parent held health and education cards might help to counteract these disruptions.

Finding an interpreter

Difficulties in finding an interpreter, especially for less common languages can prevent an adequate initial assessment of educational needs and lead to long delays in assessing a child with problems.

Problems in accessing Educational Psychologists

The services of Educational Psychologists have to be bought in, and schools have limited budgets and so are reluctant to refer early. Educational Psychologists do not have time to give informal advice about assessment and management so that only if a full statementing procedure is going ahead will they get involved, and even then only when they have reached stage 3 of the process. Thus the structure of services prevents proactive work.

To avoid this lack of proactive work one LEA, wishing to make better use of the skills of Educational Psychologists, divided them into two groups – one that did statementing and one that did more therapeutic work. This provided individual schools with the possibility of calling on someone for advice about a child's behaviour or learning at an early stage. Long delays in assessment and statementing can lead to suspension of children from school before they have gone through the statutory four stages of statementing.

Child and family consultation teams also have long waiting lists and often do not provide emergency assessment and advice.

There is a need for better ways of accessing advice before the situation worsens. One idea would be to have a dedicated mental health team made up of health and education personnel who are experienced in work with refugees, available as a reference group that will help with assessments, give advice, and treat more complex cases. Where there are refugee support teachers in schools, they may be in a good position to mobilise support before a statementing procedure is initiated or completed.

Problems in language assessment

A shortage of speech therapists and bicultural workers limits assessment of abilities in the first language. This is especially important for young children who appear to be delayed, and can mean that children with speech, language or hearing problems are not identified.

Expectations and preconceptions by teachers

Belief in the inevitability of a silent period or the need for a period of recovery from 'trauma' sometimes leads to a wait and see approach and delay in identifying the need for help, whether for emotional problems or difficulties in learning.

Resistance to statementing and to working with psychologists and psychiatrists also exists amongst some teachers. Understandably they are trying not to label or stigmatise their pupils, but at the same time they may deprive them of relevant assessment and advice.

Teachers may not identify learning or language problems in refugee children partly because of low expectations and therefore not recognise when children are achieving far below their potential. Many refugee parents have high expectations of their children and consider that the school does not expect enough, for example homework is not set regularly, or they are told that English is progressing well but then find that it is inadequate for GCSE. It is suggested that conversational English is usually fluent after about two years, but that 'academic' English takes several more years to develop.

Attitudes of parents and children

Parents refuse help because they worry about stigmatisation or think their child is being called 'mad' or 'backward'. It is difficult for them to understand the role of Educational Psychologists if they have not come across one before. A link worker, teacher or another person from their community who speaks their language and can discuss the issues with the parents and child can be very helpful in this situation.

Children hide their difficulties because they do not want to upset their parents, are ashamed of their slow learning or because they do not know there might be some help available to them. Many children who are bullied do not tell anyone because they are afraid it will make matters worse or because in the past they have found that action taken to help them and stop the bullying was ineffective.

Refugee children often worry about their progress and about failing exams, but their concerns might be justified and it is important for them to have realistic appraisals of their progress, as well as help in overcoming gaps.

❏ EDUCATIONAL AND LANGUAGE ASSESSMENT

As well as considering the effects of adversity when a child has behavioural or emotional difficulties, progress in English and education should still be assessed. It is recognised that assessment of under-achievement is challenging and requires good interpreters and adequate tests and these are not always easily accessible. The following is an outline of the areas that need to be covered in an assessment.

Development

A history of early development, especially of language, may be difficult to obtain, especially when there has been a change of carer. However, comparisons in the past may have indicated to the carers that the index child was slower than other children in the family.

Assessment of language and learning

This should include:

- a history of language acquisition. Because of frequent moves during early childhood a child may have been exposed to several different languages, and this can complicate language acquisition for the child with poor language skills, as can several languages being spoken at home

- assessment of first language abilities using a good interpreter or bicultural worker, in order to exclude a problem of general learning or a specific language difficulty

- education history including schools attended, language(s) of instruction, literacy in own language

- English attainment – current level of understanding, speaking, reading and writing English

- Current achievements in other areas if necessary assessed in first language

- school environment: bullying, racism, friendships, available support in English and school work, homework

- attendance: coming late, absences, truanting,

Parents' education

- previous education and level of literacy in their language

- knowledge of English

- involvement and understanding of school; ability to help with English at home

❏ BEHAVIOURAL ASSESSMENT

Family factors

- Who the child is living with; who has responsibility for the child

- Where the rest of family are

Changes of caretaker

- Who the child's main carers have been and are now

Social and Family tensions

- Housing, asylum status, ill health, finance, racism, safety in house and neighbourhood

- Family members' past experiences of violence, death, flight, moves, separations

Adequacy of care

- Family relations, tensions, discipline, care

- Communication within the family, family secrets,

Past experience of child

- Past experience of violence, death, flight, moves, separations

Health problems

- General health, sensory problems-hearing, vision

- Injuries

Past behavioural difficulties

Behaviour at home

- Sleep, nightmares, fears, appetite, mood, concentration

- Obedience, anger, fights

- Friends, play and interests

- Onset of difficulties

The assessment helps to answer questions about the nature of a child's difficulties and make a plan of help. Frequently a problem is multifaceted and several factors are contributory.

Considerations to be answered by an assessment are:

- the degree of handicap caused – how severely the child is suffering emotionally and socially, or in capacity to progress in school work

- are there problems in language or learning that need help in their own right?

- are behaviour or emotional difficulties related to other factors such as family tensions, events in the past, learning difficulties, school factors, worries about asylum status, or health of self or parents?

- is the child tormented 'inside' with confusion, sadness, anxiety, anger, arising from current predicaments or past adversity, conflicts over identity and loyalty?

Such a detailed assessment may only be appropriate or necessary if a child has marked difficulties, and not all this information can be found out initially. It will only be obtained after a situation of trust has developed over time, and, when the parents do not speak English, with the help of an interpreter, link worker or bicultural worker.

QUESTIONS FOR DISCUSSION

What factors lead you to think a child needs further assessment?

How could delays in assessing refugee children be shortened?

Case example

Azra, aged 10, is a girl who is very quiet and has no real friends. She has been in the country for a year but her English is still rather poor and she is not progressing well in learning. She lives with her mother and two brothers aged 12 and 6 months. The family come from Iraq and it is not known whether her father is in prison or dead.

What are the areas you would want to assess?

Chapter 14

GIVING EXTRA HELP

Decisions about support will depend on the kinds of difficulty identified. This may be based in school or require referring on for more specialist help. If children are not settling in class perhaps they are not being adequately supported at school or they are having learning difficulties; or they may be getting inadequate support at home because of pressure on the adults, and this could be remedied by work with the carers. Diverse kinds of support are required, and specialist services are not always indicated.

Schools are now initiating actions that can support children who are showing distress. These could take the form of extra attention in class from an individual teacher, a homework club or other group setting such as lunchtime groups, or individual work with a child. Even children who are very distressed may be best helped by a supportive teacher or support worker in school. Often these are the best people to help because the child knows and trusts them, and contact is informal and less threatening than referral to a clinic. It also enables support to be given when carers do not want to be involved.

The rigorous application of anti-bullying policies is also given high priority, with regular follow-up to ensure that the bullying has stopped. Many children are taught to stand up for themselves if they are insulted, because anything that affects their honour requires retaliation. When they do not have enough English to protest they may respond with physical aggression.

❏ PEER SUPPORT
Peer support ranges from befriending schemes especially during the induction period, to peer counselling initiatives in which there is considerable preparation and supervision of the counsellors.

❑ SMALL GROUP WORK

Some children feel very threatened by the closeness of one-to-one relationships and prefer group activities. These can be carried out through tutorial classes which provide moral support as well as specific help with English or other subjects. Possible activities are writing exercises (perhaps in their first language initially), oral history projects, and drama.

Homework clubs help children who have no room to work at home and may also provide a place where discussions and group solidarity can develop.

An opportunity to get together regularly with others of a particular age group can also be helpful. For example adolescent girls in this situation might initially discuss issues such as English and homework, and bullying, and then move on to doubts about their future related to intergenerational issues, work and marriage.

❑ ASSESSMENT AND MAKING A PLAN

Assessment in itself can be all that is needed – simply by bringing people together to review difficulties and making plans for support or change.

> A Kurdish girl, Sara, aged nearly 5, had never been to school before and was very restless in school. She would not sit down but wandered around the classroom looking at everything and seeming confused. She spoke quite a lot but it was in a language that nobody understood.
>
> Careful assessment of her language found that it was a garbled mixture of Turkish and Kurdish; she had been exposed to both these languages. At home her parents spoke mainly Turkish and some Kurdish and English.
>
> A discussion was held with the parents about how best to meet Sara's language needs and help her to settle into school, and the following plan was made:
>
> • to keep her in the nursery class for an extra year so she could get used to the school setting
>
> • allow her time to become accustomed to school before gradually involving her in more formal learning activities in the classroom
>
> • that her parents would speak only Turkish to her at home for the present

❑ LISTENING AND SUPPORTING

Talking to a child can elucidate difficulties and lead to a plan for dealing with them.

> It was noted that Jamal, aged 10 and formerly a good pupil, was now coming late to school and no longer completed his homework; he became withdrawn from his friends.

His teacher talked to him confidentially, and found that he had just heard that his father had been killed.

His teacher discussed with Jamal's mother the sadness of their loss and indicated how she (the teacher) could help. She made sure she had a brief word with him every day and did not pressurise him in class, understanding that at times he could not concentrate or that he wanted to be alone.

She discussed with him whether he wanted to tell his friends about his father and he said he would tell just two good friends but did not want the whole class to know.

Over the weeks Jamal gradually became less distressed and told his teacher that he was now able to concentrate and enjoy school again.

I'm not sad any more

❑ ASSESSMENT AND MANAGEMENT

Assessment may can done in conjunction with some specialist input, followed by support mainly in the school setting.

Sanya was a 13 year old Bosnian girl, living with her aunt and uncle and their two young children; they have been in this country for about eighteen months. Her father was killed fighting in Bosnia and her mother was still in Sarajevo.

Sanya was not happy in school. She had not made friends and her progress in English was slow. At home she was miserable and irritable. The family had ELR.

An assessment was carried out at the local Child and Adolescent Mental Health Team (CAMHT) with Sanya and the rest of her family. The interpreter was the school link worker, a Bosnian already known to Sanya.

The following factors that might be upsetting Sanya were explored:

- missing her mother and mourning her father

- worring about safety of other relatives in Sarajevo

- feeling she needs more attention at home

- being unable to concentrate on school work because she is preoccupied by her anxieties and sadness

- having learning difficulties

- finding her school mates unfriendly

- feeling too sad to make friends with others

- feeling that the class teacher is not sympathetic

- being upset by memories of violence

- feeling guilty about 'deserting' her friends in Bosnia

It was felt that Sanya did not have learning difficulties but was not concentrating well because she had not had the chance to mourn her father's death or to express her feelings about leaving her mother behind in Sarajevo. The aunt and uncle had not discussed this with her as they did not want to distress her more.

A plan was made to help Sanya through the following steps:

- a second meeting at the CAMHT to encourage the family to recognise their mutual feelings of sadness

- Sanya met weekly for one term to talk over her difficulties and feelings with the school link worker who was supervised by the borough's refugee project coordinator, and who maintained contact with her afterwards

- the class teacher ensured that Sanya was not left out of activities and projects. The other girls had thought she was unfriendly because she was withdrawn

- the school involved her in a music project as this was a great interest of hers and she sang well

In this way her self-esteem was improved, she was integrated into the class and was more able to express her feelings. At a follow up three months later she had made some friends and felt that she was now mastering her lessons.

The presence of a supportive family and the care given by her uncle and aunt were also important positive factors in her progress.

❏ REFERRAL FOR SPECIALIST HELP

Certain factors make it advisable to have specialists involved at least during the assessment period. These are indicated as headings, below.

Persistent unhappiness

This can be related to:

lack of a supportive relationship at home or sadness about the death or absence of important figures

previous experiences of violence or abuse especially sexual abuse, which may go unreported by the child

bullying at school or difficulties in learning

Case for discussion

Ahmed, a 4 year old boy, came to this country from Somalia with his sister one year ago. In the classroom he did not speak or sit down but wandered around and ignored the other children. He did not seem to be learning English. At times he was aggressive when forced to do something he did not want to do, but he seemed generally unhappy.

What do you think might be the causes of this boy's difficulties?

What would you need to know in order to assess the situation?

It was found that Ahmed's mother had died when he was 2 years old and since then he had been looked after by his sister. She was unable to give a clear picture of his early development but thought it had been normal, and that at home he spoke normally. He had never been to school in Somalia.

During their flight from Somalia they had a very frightening time, and the sister was still extremely distressed by her experiences of violence and rape, and finding it difficult to respond to Ahmed's needs.

Currently they were very isolated and their uncertain asylum situation was giving rise to much anxiety.

It was not possible to assess Ahmed's mother-tongue capacities at the first assessment because he did not speak at all. It was noted that he was an alert child who was exploring puzzles and toys up to his age level.

Following a hearing test there was a query about a hearing loss and this was going to be assessed again.

It was felt that Ahmed's problems were probably caused by a mixture of factors including his sister's continuing distress, his frightening journey to Britain, a possible hearing loss that needed careful monitoring, and unfamiliarity with school

Plans to help him were:

- individual attention and small group work in school so that he could form a relationship with a special needs teacher and receive extra help with English

- support from his class teacher to help him feel safe in school and integrate him with a small group of other children

- support for his sister first individually and then in a group, to help her to come to terms with her experiences of violence, adapt to her new environment, learn English, and meet other people with similar experiences.

Threats of or attempts at suicide, or self harm

Some young people in desperation take overdoses or injure themselves. Often these are cries for help arising out of depression or fear of being deported. Young people in detention are especially at risk because of the tension under which they are living.

> An Algerian young man slashed his arms with a razor after being in detention for some months with no idea what was going to happen to him. He was terrified of being deported because he was sure his life would be at risk if he returned to Algeria.

Prolonged and severe difficulties in conduct

Children who are aggressive may have experienced violence prior to exile and occasionally have been personally involved in violent acts. Other causes of violence are bullying, depression, abuse at home, and failing in schoolwork.

Children with conduct disorder may be suspended or even expelled from school without a proper assessment. It may be assumed that they cannot be helped in school, yet if the factors contributing to their behaviour were understood it could well be that they could be helped, preventing the secondary adversity of expulsion being added to the primary adversities of loss and violence.

Bizarre behaviour

Some refugee children exhibit strange behaviour: relating poorly to others, rushing aimlessly around, not being able to concentrate on anything for more than a few seconds, disrupting games and hitting others without provocation. This kind of behaviour tends to occur in younger children, especially those who have not been to school before, and who are bewildered by what is expected of them and what is happening around them. These children do not necessarily have severe learning difficulties or a severe psychological disturbance although clearly these possibilities must be borne in mind.

> Abshir at age 6 was agitated, disruptive and hyperactive at school and hardly learning anything. He seemed to be affected by his parent's separation which led

> to living only with his father and limited contact with his mother. His father was not responding to him well, whereas his mother seemed to be attentive and more in touch with his needs

Children may show very disturbed behaviour when they are agitated by tensions at home or changes of carer which add to their apprehension. Lack of adequate care can arise because of the death of or separation from one or both parents, loss of the main carer, frequent changes of carer, abuse and neglect.

Parenting difficulties

Parenting difficulties can arise because of current tensions over asylum, social conditions, or family left behind, when anxiety makes it difficult for parents to be calm and responsive to their children. Parents who are easily irritated because of their past experiences of violence and torture find it hard to cope with the inevitable noisiness and demands of children. They have probably been used to letting the children play outside, which is not possible in this climate or because of a risky neighbourhood. Being stuck at home in cramped conditions adds to family tensions.

Young children respond to parents' irritability and inconsistency with behaviour difficulties such as outbursts of temper, disobedience, and eating problems. Issues of discipline also arise with older children who want to stay out late or copy their peers in dress or behaviour.

Depressed and distressed parents may be unable to care adequately for their children, who in fact may take over the parental role.

In extreme situations neglect, physical or sexual abuse may lead to a child being taken into care (see Chapter 15).

It is helpful for parents to discuss, either in a group or individually, how best to manage these problems, and how they can bring up their children in this new environment.

Risk of leaving home

Family tensions, conflicts with parents, generational issues affect older children, especially girls. When these conflicts show no sign of being resolved the young person may run away from home.

Girls who are being pressurised to conform, to leave school and start work, or to agree to an early arranged marriage, may become depressed.

QUESTIONS FOR DISCUSSION

What criteria would you use for referring a child for specialist help?

Case studies

Cesaire, a 12 year old boy from Zaire, is aggressive and restless in school. He has a few friends and enjoys sports but not academic work, and is sometimes absent from school for no apparent reason. He lives with an older brother, aged 21, with whom he argues a lot.

What might be the causes of his difficulties at home and at school?

How could the school help him?

Fatma, a Kurdish girl aged 15, has been in secondary school for two years. She is depressed and having difficulties in learning and doing her home-work. What are the various factors that might be affecting her at home and at school? She lives with her parents and 16 year old brother.

In what ways might she be helped?

Chapter 15

CHILDREN IN CARE

Child protection is always a sensitive issue, dealing as it does with the rights of children and the rights of parents, difficulties in arriving at the 'truth', the need to consider all the possible long term results of removing a child from home, as well as the complexities of providing adequate alternative care (Social Services Inspectorate, 1995).

Where a refugee child is concerned these dilemmas are magnified for various reasons:

- obstacles to communication and understanding between clients and helpers, especially in establishing trust and mutual respect

- cultural differences in child rearing and in family life

- the complexity of identity development in refugee children and how this is affected by removal from home

- difficulties in finding alternative carers for children removed from home

- difficulties in working with families and in carrying out preventive work

- potential conflicts between asylum law and child care law. Legislation about children, in particular the Children Act of 1989, is not always consonant with asylum legislation, and this raises clinical and ethical issues about how to respond to refugee children. Threats of deportation and barriers to family reunification for children who have ELR may not be consonant with the best needs of a child as determined by the Children Act.

❑ COMMUNICATION AND UNDERSTANDING

A significant obstacle in communication lies in the complexity of reaching a mutual understanding with families about causes for concern and about the role of social services. We must not underestimate the blocks to communication arising from lack of trust, especially of officials, in people who have lived in repressive and violent societies. Refugees fear that any information they give might be misused, especially when their asylum situation is precarious and they fear that confidentiality will not be preserved. Their distrust makes them unwilling to give information and this increases difficulties in assessing parenting.

The current moves to expand preventive social work could be an impetus to improving mutual understanding and reduce the suspicion of social services that exists amongst refugees.

❏ ASSESSING PARENTING AND CULTURAL DIFFERENCES

World wide there are marked cultural differences in what is seen as good parenting, for example in the degree of responsibility given to children, in the way they are communicated with, in the use of physical punishment. We need to consider carefully how to respond to these differences; this is to protect the child but also to recognise that what is thought to be wrong or neglectful in this society is seen differently in other communities.

We should neither idealise nor disparage British culture or the cultures of other societies but focus instead on whether the needs of children are being acknowledged and met, and how to assess this. Assessment has to take into account the effects on parents or other carers of their experiences of organised violence and of life in exile, and the immediate and longer term needs of families in which both parents and children have suffered serious adversity.

Respecting parents

Parents who cannot speak English and are under the strain of adapting to a strange land, are not always treated with respect by professionals. It is all too easy to ally with the child during an investigation of suspected physical abuse and further undermine the already threatened status in the family of the parents. This happens for example when parents have not informed a child about the deaths of relatives, because they are believed in their culture to be too young to cope with this information. Sometimes professionals insist on the child being told, against the parents' wishes, rather than deferring the decision to inform the child and finding a time more suited to the family's culture.

> A social worker insisted on telling a child her mother was dead although the father wished the news to be delayed. The way the news was broken affected the child's trust in her father, and was experienced as deeply humiliating for the father.

There is a risk of overlooking the fact that the majority of parents have acted wisely to keep their children safe, and show great strength in coping with life in exile.

❏ CAUSES OF COMING INTO CARE

Refugee children arrive into care through a number of pathways.

Unaccompanied children

Children are considered to be unaccompanied if there is no adult to take full responsibility for them, or if they are being cared for by someone who would not normally do so.

Unaccompanied children arrive either completely alone or with another person or family, who may or may not be known to the child, and who usually leave them immediately on arrival. In 1997 around 600 unaccompanied children arrived in the United Kingdom, and the rate of arrivals is going up. In 1997 only 8% were granted full refugee status, and 52% were given ELR; the remaining 40% were refused.

Reasons for leaving their country are various. Some are sent away to safety or to avoid conscription, or they became accidentally separated from their families. Others belong to families who are targeted by those in authority or other armed groups. In some cases many members of the family have already been killed, and the young person does not know if any are still living. Their histories of flight often tell of prolonged and dangerous journeys. Some of the unaccompanied girls have had horrendous experiences of flight, capture and multiple rape.

> Yolande arrived as an unaccompanied girl of 16. She knew that her father and two brothers had been killed but did not know whether any of her other siblings had survived. She had been raped and beaten.

Many young people flee because they are caught between government and insurgent forces and are at risk because, although they want to be neutral, both sides see them as adversaries.

Evacuation from war zones for safety or for medical treatment or even for holidays, as happened with some children from Bosnia, can leave children stranded, with no possibility of returning home for a long time because of the war situation. UNHCR (1994) advises that evacuation for whatever reason should be done with caution, because children without parents are more distressed that those remaining with their families even if this exposes them to danger (Raphael, 1986). Once families are separated reunification often becomes problematic.

Unaccompanied refugee children are particularly vulnerable since they have lost both their family and their culture. They are homesick, and in the case of some of the younger children even uncertain about why they were sent out of the country.

Breakdown of care arrangements at home

The disruptive experiences of oppression and uprooting inevitably lead to substantial changes in family structure: families are reconstituted and children are faced with unknown step-parents or placed with relatives they have never lived with and may never even have met before. The family may be living in overcrowded housing, and have other social difficulties. Not surprisingly, there may be tensions in these new family units: children are resentful of new partners or unaccepting of discipline, and the situation breaks down.

Other carers, such as a slightly older brother, sister or aunt, are themselves young and inexperienced and are trying to adapt to their new situation. Frequently these young relatives do not have the experience to care properly for a young teenager, and the pressures on them are so great that they cannot respond to their young relative's needs. Where carers are themselves young they need special support to care for a child or adolescent, who in turn may require extra backing if they are to feel secure.

> Mohammed aged 14 was sent by his family to stay with an older brother. In fact he had never met this brother before, because he had lived in a different place and fled from the country three years previously. The two brothers did not get on and after a few months Mohammed asked to be placed separately.

Children who leave home

Intergenerational conflict leads some children to leave home, Girls are particularly affected because of the restrictions on their freedom. If a girl is even seen talking to a boy she may be considered dishonoured and beaten by the males in her family. Some girls leave home because life is so restricted and they are made unhappy by the constant arguments about dress, going out and curfews.

Often conflicts arise because the generations are adapting differently to their situation. Children are more integrated into the host culture; adults find integration more problematic. This can create increasing distance between the generations, with parents desperately trying to protect their children from the alien mores of the host culture, and children becoming antagonised by this.

Death and parental illness

Not having an extended family puts children at risk when their carer becomes ill or dies.

John thought his parents had been killed and was able to escape here, where his brother was already living. However the brother was ill with AIDS and died after two years. John was having difficulties with his asylum claim because he did not have all the details of his brother's claim and became depressed and withdrawn.

Child protection and abuse

Differences in child rearing practices often cause mutual dismay for refugees and hosts, particularly about physical punishment, condemned in this country but considered an essential part of good child care in many places. Accusations of child abuse often surprise families criticised for hitting their children. Their view of childhood may be that parents (or guardians) are in charge of their children and the state has no right to interfere with their control. Parents are at a loss as to how else they are supposed to discipline their children.

Sometimes children are aware that if they complain about physical punishment they will be taken into care and they may use this to blackmail their carers into giving them things or relaxing discipline. Whilst not condoning physical abuse or neglect, we need to understand these different attitudes to child rearing and to aim at preventing problems by discussing the issues with refugee communities.

When abuse has occurred it may be difficult to assess the strength of attachment between parent and child and whether it is advisable to take the child into care.

> A boy of 6, Faisal, was taken into care after telling a neighbour that his older siblings who had responsibility for him were beating him up. On assessment it was found that the family had suffered a great deal in their flight into exile and were generally very tense. They were attached to Faisal and in fact spoilt him, but they did hit him when he was naughty, sometimes harshly, and he was often quite provocative.

What should be done in this situation?

> Faisal remained in care only briefly and was then returned home. It was discussed with the family how they might deal with their own tensions, but they remained uncertain about how they could discipline Faisal and they needed more help with working this out.

Leaving older children in charge of younger siblings is acceptable in communities where neighbours are known and children are used to responsibility, but this is not acceptable in Britain.

> On one occasion three children were taken into care when a neighbour informed social services that they had been left by the parents who had gone to the Housing Department. The eldest child was 10 years old. When the parents returned home the children had been taken into care.

This raises the issue of how best to manage such a situation, taking into account the best interests of the children, who might well be terrified at being removed by strangers especially as their English was poor.

❑ HELPING CHILDREN IN CARE

Unaccompanied children

Whatever the reason for seeking asylum it is unlikely that there has been much preparation for the separation; often departure has to be a hurried affair with no time for goodbyes. Parents do not always explain to children why they are sending them away. Youngsters may view the journey as an exciting adventure, only to find the reality of separation shattering.

Unaccompanied children need continuity of care but changes of social workers, care workers, or breakdown of foster care, can lead to discontinuity and afford no chance to build up any lasting relationships. Almost certainly they have never lived alone before and independence is lonely and frightening, especially for those placed in lodgings on their own. Anxiety over asylum increases their vulnerability.

Home Office paid advisers are assigned through the Refugee Council to unaccompanied children when they arrive to ensure that they are receiving adequate care and proper legal representation. The advisers are important sources of support for newly arrived unaccompanied refugees, but currently their contact is supposed to stop as soon as refugee status or ELR has been granted. The ending of what has become an important relationship is distressing for some young people.

Housing

Initial placement may be in a children's home or a hostel or in bed and breakfast. Or for those over sixteen it can mean living alone in a flat. Some wish to live on their own but others find this extremely depressing.

Some young people who are on their own and feel unable to cope with their situation become very depressed and even suicidal. This is even worse once they reach 18 years of age and no longer receive any social services support. The needs of older refugee adolescents for a home and a caring relationship are frequently overlooked. They need preparation for independence, especially with managing money and time, recreational clubs, facilities for learning English.

In a few cases hostels have been provided for unaccompanied refugee children, eg for a group of Vietnamese children who were cared for by social workers. This setting provided them with a more family type setting and with moral support, and is possibly a helpful solution for some refugees. However many unaccompanied young people would certainly do better in foster care if it were possible to organise it. It has also been suggested that hostels would be helpful for young people who leave home, and would probably help to maintain family contact as this solution would be more acceptable to them than a foster home or the young person living alone.

❏ FINDING ALTERNATIVE CARERS

Children in care are at increased risk of psychological difficulties. This is partly related to the adverse experiences that lead them into care and, possibly, partly to unsatisfactory experiences in care. For refugee children it is doubly harsh to lose not only familiar carers but also a familiar cultural context.

Foster parents that come from the same background as the refugee children are hard to find. The need to 'match' foster carers and what this implies must be clarified. In the past it has sometimes been assumed that matching skin colour is sufficient to deal with cultural differences, but this has ignored great differences in culture, for example between people from different African countries. There are now initiatives to look for foster parents that match the cultural background of refugee children, and to offer them support and back-up.

The long term effects on children's identity of removal from home must be considered. Moving children to a placement that is not of their own culture can have a potent effect on their identity. They may hold aloof from the new family and perhaps cause the placement to break down. Or they may want to affiliate strongly with a new family that provides security and affection and this can lead them to distance themselves from their own culture, while having feelings of disloyalty and guilt about their own family.

Moving children to a new home with possibly a higher standard of living may further alienate them from their origins and exacerbate the difficulties of reconciliation.

❏ WORKING WITH FAMILIES

Assessment

Assessment must focus on deciding whether the child is at risk of injury, the quality of care, the strength of attachment between carer(s) and child, whether it is possible to work with parents.

The emotional state of the caretakers must also be considered. How are they affected by the past (losses, separation, violence) and by their current situation? Communication in the family and whether they have secrets from one another are also important.

It must be recognised that refugee children who are estranged from their families are also likely to lose contact with their communities, and run the risk of feeling rootless and alone.

If at all possible the aim should be to help the young person return to their family or at the least maintain links with them.

Hostility by parents towards social workers may be related to the following factors:

- poor understanding of the role of social workers; fear that their children are going to be taken away for ever

- not understanding why their behaviour is unacceptable

- trying to deny that they use physical punishment

The social worker might exacerbate problems if they

- have preconceptions about refugees eg assume that they are inadequate parents

- have little respect for the parents

- do not try to get a full picture of the family situation, and all the antecedent or current factors affecting them

When children are removed from home it is essential to maintain links with families as far as possible.

Reunification

In planning care for unaccompanied children the 1989 Children Act should take priority over asylum law, eg in dealing with housing needs or pressing for reunification. Reunification ought to be a priority for young children but this is not always accepted by authorities. In many cases even if the whereabouts of relatives is known it is not possible for them to get permission to enter this country even for a visit.

❑ PSYCHOLOGICAL SUPPORT

Unaccompanied children require the presence of a caring adult to replace their lost carers and ease the transition into their new life. Unfortunately because many of them are in their later teens it may be thought that they can manage more or less independently. Youths as young as sixteen have been placed in bed and breakfast accommodation or in flats on their own with little social support. Some unaccompanied children isolate themselves from their community because they are suspicious of the affiliations of others and this makes them more isolated.

The Panel of Advisers now organised by the Refugee Council only provide support until asylum status is finalised, but it is possible that the role of the advisers may be extended to give support for longer.

For some young people social work after-care programmes continue after a young person turns 18, but for others care stops abruptly. However they are usually without an adequate social network or finances and this sudden change of circumstances can be devastating. Isolation can lead to depression and sometimes suicidal feelings, as well as difficulties with learning. If there is no certainty about whether any family have survived this adds to their desolation.

Some of these isolated youths would benefit from placement in a foster home or a hostel for groups of refugees from the same country which could promote a sense of group identity. Other possibilities of help are befriending schemes either from their own community or the host community, in which a 'big brother' or an 'aunt and uncle' provide a stable relationship.

Group activities through youth or sports clubs, or community centres might also help to integrate these young people socially. Individual help because of depression and loneliness may be required – possibly in conjunction with a therapeutic group – before they feel able to join in ordinary social activities.

- assessment and helping children with psychological difficulties

- networking

Support, in the context of a normal, secure life and a responsive educational system, has an important preventive element through averting secondary adversit, and promoting confidence and achievement. School policies are important: they should cover eliminating racism and bullying, promoting English language teaching, and linking effectively with parents.

When children are not settled this is often related to their current social or educational conditions, to secondary adversities or, most importantly, to loss or separation from their main carer(s). Consequently unaccompanied children are most vulnerable, even if they have not suffered directly from violence.

Protective work for unaccompanied children involves ensuring a satisfactory caring situation, adequate housing, a stable relationship with a caring person, appropriate schooling. For most young people after-care is needed after 16 years of age and often for a few years subsequently, if they are to become fully settled.

Children are less confused if they are able to integrate their past and present experiences and if they have the opportunity to talk about them. They will be helped to develop a 'bicultural' identity if they find the host culture accepting, and are able to maintain links with and value their own culture and language. The process of integration inevitably takes time but it is greatly helped by adults who are culturally sensitive. Training community bicultural workers as interpreters, teachers, social workers, home school link workers, counsellors, etc. has a significant effect. The presence of people from their own communities supports the children's culture, provides adult role models, and raises the status of refugees.

Identifying and planning for children with serious difficulties is often delayed, with the result that children lose hope and the situation escalates. Early assessment and initiation of specific help can halt this downward spiral, but such provision is often hindered by lack of adequate services and sometimes by unnecessary postponement of seeking help.

The existence of a designated local mental health team would have a number of advantages. It could develop institutional experience in assessment and treatment that can be passed on to others and provide assessment, advice and therapy in complex cases, and also training and supervision.

Although this book has focused on the difficulties and problems encountered by refugees, I would like to emphasise again that the majority of refugees have come from caring homes and have developed strategies for dealing with adversity and show impressive capacities to cope. However, even these children need a supportive environment, especially if they have encountered great hardship.

In spite of all they have been through, many refugees show impressive strength – optimism about the future, a wish to learn and make friends, and a capacity to support their parents and brothers and sisters.

QUESTIONS FOR DISCUSSION

What are your training needs for working with refugee children?

How could you meet these needs?

What training could you organise for others?

REFERENCES

Abdullah R. and Benjamin J. (1995) *Somali health needs assessment in the London borough of Hackney, an initial exploration.* Community Psychiatry Research Unit, City and Hackney Community Services NHS Trust.

Africa Watch (1990) *Somalia. A Government at War with its Own People.* Africa Watch Report

Arroyo W. and Eth S. (1985) Children Traumatised by Central American Warfare, in R. Pynoos and S. Eth (eds) *Post-traumatic stress disorder in children.* American Psychiatric Association

Barudy J. (1989) A programme of mental health for political refugees: dealing with the political pain of exile. *Social Science and Medicine* 28, 715-727

Beattie S. (1994) Lifeline: the Education of young survivors of war and violent oppression. In K. Price (ed) *Community Support for Survivors of Torture: a manual.* Toronto, Canadian Centre for Victims of Torture.

Blakeney J., Jama Dirie F., and Macrae M.A. (1994) Empowering Traumatised Somali Women. A support group model for helping survivors to cope. In K. Price (ed) *Community Support for Survivors of Torture: a manual.* Toronto, Canadian Centre for Victims of Torture.

Bolloten B. and Spafford T. (1996) *Teaching Refugee Children; a guide to resources.* Newham English Language Service INSEC. The Credon Centre, Kirton Road, E13 9DR

Boman B. and Edwards M. (1984) The Indochina refugee: an overview. *Australian and New Zealand Journal of Psychiatry.* 18, 40-62

Brown C., Barnfield J., Stone M. (1991) *Spanner in the Works; education for racial equality and social justice in white schools.* Stoke on Trent, Trentham Books

Camden Language and Support Service Refugee Team (1994) Horn of Africa After School Project

Camden Refugee Students Writing Group (1995) Health Checklist for Staff Working with Refugee Children in Camden Schools

Carey-Wood J., Duke K., Karn V. and Marshall T. (1995) *The Settlement of Refugees in Britain*, London, HMSO

Croall J (1995) 'Children of the Storm' *Guardian Education* May 2nd

Cummins, J. (1984) *Bilingualism and special education.* Clevedon, Multilingual Matters

Dagnino N. (1992) Responding to the Psychosocial Needs of Refugee Children: a Multifaceted Approach. In M. McCallin (ed) *The Psychological Well-Being of Refugee Children; research, practice and policy issues.* International Catholic Child Bureau, Geneva

Dalglish C.A. (1989) *Refugees from Vietnam.* London, Macmillan

Daycare Trust Report (ed C.Sherriff)(1995) Touching First Base. Meeting the Needs of Refugee Children and Families from the Horn of Africa

Dwivedi K.N. (1995) Social Structures that Support or Undermine Families from Ethnic Minority Groups: Eastern Value Systems. In *Context. Ethnicity, Culture, Race and Family Therapy.* Association for Family Therapy. Hants., Basingstoke Press

Eastmond M. (1989) The Dilemmas of Exile. Chilean Refugees in the USA. PhD. University of Gothenburg

Edwards V. (1998) *The Power of Babel – teaching and learning in multilingual classrooms.* Stoke on Trent, Trentham Books

Eisenbruch M. (1991) From Post-traumatic Stress Disorder to Cultural Bereavement: diagnosis of Southeast Asian refugees. *Social Science and Medicine.* 30, 673-680

Finlay R. and Reynolds J. (eds.) (1987) *Children from Refugee Communities. A question of identity: uprooting, integration or dual culture.* London, Refugee Action

Freire M. (1994) Children and Repression: issues for child care workers and school personnel. In K. Price (ed) *Community Support for Survivors of Torture: a manual.* Toronto, Canadian Centre for Victims of Torture.

Furedi F. (1997) *Culture of Fear.* London Cassell

George Mitchell School. Why? – a Video by year 7 George Mitchell School. Waltham Forest Media Resource Unit, George Mitchell School.

Gorst-Unsworth C. and Goldenberg E. (1998) Psychological sequelae of torture and organised violence suffered by refugees from Iraq. *British Journal of Psychiatry* 172, 90-94

Hendessi M. (1987) *Migrants: The Invisible Homeless. A report on migrants' housing needs and circumstances in London.* Migrant services Unit, London Voluntary Service Council

Hewitt M. and Harris A. (1991) *Talking Time! A Guide to Oral History for Schools. Learning by Design,* Tower Hamlets Education.

Hoffman E. (1989) *Lost in Translation,* London, Minerva

Jones C. and Rutter J. (1998) *Refugee Education: mapping the field.* Stoke on Trent, Trentham Books.

Kansu F. (1997) *Assessing the Health Needs of Turkish and Kurdish Speaking Women in Hackney.* Open Doors Sexual Health Project, St. Leonards Primary Care, Nuttall Street London N1 5LZ

Kareem J. and Littlewood R. (eds) (1992) *Intercultural Therapy.* Oxford, Blackwell

Keilson H. (1992) *Sequential Traumatization in Children.* Jerusalem, Magnes Press

Lau A. (1995) Gender, Culture and Family Life. In *Context. Ethnicity, Culture, Race and Family Therapy.* Association for Family Therapy. Hants., Basingstoke Press

Leibkind K. (1983) Self-reported ethnic identity, depression and anxiety among young Vietnamese refugees and their parents. *Journal of Refugee Studies* 6, 25-39.

Lewis I.M. (1994) *Blood and Bone; the call of kinship in Somali society.* Lawrenceville, Red Sea Press

Lin K-M., Masuda M. and Tazuma L. (1982) Problems of Vietnamese Refugees in the US in R.C. Nann (ed) *Uprooting and Surviving.* Dordrecht, Reidel

Littlewood R. and Lipsedge M. (1989) *Aliens and Alienists; Ethnic Minorities and Psychiatry.* London, Unwin Hyman

Loizos P. (1981) *The Heart Grown Bitter; a chronicle of Cypriot war refugees.* Cambridge, Cambridge University Press.

Loncarevic M. (1996) 'MIR' Socio-Cultural Integration Project for Bosnian refugees. In G. Perren-Klingler (ed) *From Individual Helplessness to Group Resources,* Berne, Haupt

McCallin M. The impact of Current and Traumatic Stressors on the Psychological Well-Being of Refugee Communities. In M. McCallin (ed) *The Psychological Well-Being of Refugee Children: Research, Practice and Policy Issues.* International Catholic Child Bureau, Geneva

McDonald J. (1995) Entitled to Learn? A report on young refugees' experiences of access and progression in the UK Education System. World University Service

McDowell D. (1992) *The Kurds. A Nation Denied*. London, Minority Rights Group

Melzak S. (1992) Secrecy, Privacy, Survival, Repressive Regimes and Growing Up. Bulletin of the Anna Freud Centre 15, 205-224

Melzak S. (1995) Thinking about the internal and external experiences of refugee children in Europe. In Stifftung fur Kinder/UNICEF (eds) *Children, War and Persecution*. Osnabruck, Secolo Verlag

Melzak S. and Warner R. (1992) Integrating Refugee Children into Schools. Minority Rights Group

Munoz L. (1980) Exile as bereavement: Socio-psychological manifestations of Chilean exiles in Great Britain. *British Journal of Medical Psychology*. 53, 227-232

Nguyen A.N. and Williams H.L. (1989) Transition from East to West: Vietnamese adolescents and their parents. *Journal of the American Academy of Child and Adolescent Psychiatry*, 28, 505-515

O'Brian C. (1995) Strangers in a Strange Land: European Ethnic Minority Families at Risk. In Context. Ethnicity, Culture, Race and Family Therapy. Association for Family Therapy. Hants., Basingstoke Press

Parkes C.M., Laungani P. and Young B. (1997) *Death and Bereavement across Cultures*. London, Routledge

Peer Counselling Networker (1996) Department of Psychology, Roehampton Institute London

Power S., Whitty G. and Youdell D. (1995) No place to learn. Homelessness and Education. London, Shelter

Raphael B. (1986) *When Disaster Strikes*. London, Unwin Hyman

Refugee Council (1997) Asylum Statistics in the UK. 1986-1996

Reichelt S. and Sveaass N. (1994) Developing meaningful conversations with families in exile. *Journal of Refugee Studies*. 7, 125-143

Richman N. (1993) Communicating with Children; Helping Children in Distress. London, Save the Children

Richman N. (1993) Annotation: Children in Situations of Political Violence. *Journal of Child Psychology and Psychiatry*. 34, 1286-1302.

Richman N. (1996) They don't recognise our dignity. A study of the psychosocial needs of children and families in Hackney. City and Hackney Community Services NHS Trust, Child and Adolescent Services

Rutter J. (1991a) *Refugees. We left because we had to. An Educational Book for 14-18 year olds*. London, Refugee Council

Rutter J. (1991b) *Refugees: a resource book for 8-13 year olds*. London, Refugee Council

Rutter J. (1994) *Refugee Children in the Classroom*. Stoke on Trent, Trentham Books

Sack W.H., Angell R.H., Kinzie J.D. and Rath B. (1986) The psychiatric effects of massive trauma on Cambodian children; II, the family, the home and the school. *Journal of the American Academy of Child Psychiatry*. 25, 377-383

Samatar S. (1991) *Somalia: a Nation in Turmoil*. London, MRG

Shackman J. (1995) The Right to be Understood. Available from J. Shackman Medical Foundation for Victims of Torture (see Appendix)

Slim H. and Thompson P. (1993) *Listening for a Change*. London, Panos

Sluzki C.E. (1989) Network disruption and network reconstruction in the process of migration/relocation. *Bulletin of the Berkshire Medical Centre* 2: 2-4

Sluzki C.E. (1994) Migration and Family Conflict. *Family Process* 8, 379-390

Social Services Inspectorate (1995) *Unaccompanied Asylum-seeking Children. A Practice Guide.* Department of Health

Summerfield D. (1995) Raising the dead: war, reparation and the politics of memory. *British Medical Journal* 311, 495-7

Tang M. (1994) Vietnamese Refugees: Towards a Healthy Future. Final Report Deptford Vietnamese Project. Save the Children/Optimum Health Services

Tattum D. and Herbert G. (1993) *Countering Bullying.* Stoke on Trent, Trentham Books

UN Convention on the Rights of the Child Geneva November, 1989

UNHCR (1994) *Refugee Children. Guidelines on Protection and Care.* Geneva

Valtonen K. (1994) Adaptation of Vietnamese refugees in Finland. *Journal of Refugee Studies.* 7:63-78

van der Veer G. (1992) *Counselling and Therapy with Refugees: psychological problems of victims of war, torture and repression.* Chichester, Wiley.

van der Veer G. (1993) Psychotherapy with Traumatised Adolescent Refugees. In Health Hazards of Organised Violence in Children: a Meeting of Advisory Group on Health Situation of Refugees and Victims of Organised Violence. London February 1993

Wagner P. and Lodge C. (1995) Refugee Children in School. National Association of Pastoral Care in Education. NAPCE Dept.of Education, University of Warwick

Warner R. (ed) (1991) *Voices from Kurdistan/Eritrea/Somalia.* London, Minority Rights Group

Warner R. (ed) (1995) *Voices from Angola/Sudan/Uganda/Zaire.* London, Minority Rights Group

Woodcock J. (1995) Family therapy with refugees and political exiles. In *Context. Ethnicity, Culture, Race and Family Therapy.* Association for Family Therapy. Hants., Basingstoke Press

Woodcock J. (1994) The Cruelty of Waiting: clinical work with refugee families who have suffered atrocity and separation. Dissertation: Advanced Clinical Training in Family Therapy

APPENDIX

Amnesty International
1 Easton Street,
London WC1X 8DJ
0171 413 5500

Children's Legal Centre
London PO BOX 3314 N1 2WA

**Directory: Mental Health
Services for Refugees**
Greater London. Refugee
Council/Mental Health Foundation

**Immigration Law Practitioners'
Association**
London 115 Old Street EC1V 9JR
0171 250 1671

**Medical Foundation for the Care
and Treatment of Victims of
Torture**
96 Grafton Road
London NW5 3EJ
0171 813 7777

Minority Rights Group
379 Brixton Road
London SW9 7DE
0171 978 9498

**Nafsiyat Intercultural Therapy
Centre**
278 Seven Sisters Road
London N4 2HY
0171 263 4130

Refugee Council
3 Bondway
London SW8 1SJ
0171 582 6922

Refugee Legal Centre
Sussex House, Bermondsey Street
London SE1 3XF
0171 827 9090

London Drama Office
Holborn Centre for the
Performing Arts
Three Cups Yard, Sandland Street
London WC1 R 4PZ
0171 405 4519
*An organisation of teachers and others
concerned with Drama and Theatre in
education.*

Leap Theatre
Leaveners Art Base
8 Lennox Road
London N4 3NW
0171 272 5630